ABCs
TO INTIMACY WITH
GOD

ABCs
TO INTIMACY WITH
GOD

Ignite
Faith, Hope, and Joy
through Worship

JEANETTE WILLIAMS

Book cover by: designer_pro247

Photos by: Audrienne 'Yonnie' Stevens, Carol Morris, Sonya Morris, and Derek Pollard

Editor: Lisa Landers

ISBN: 979-8-9880561-0-2 (e-book)
ISBN: 979-8-9880561-1-9 (print)
ISBN: 979-8-9880561-2-6 (audible)

Printed in the U. S. A.

DEDICATION

To my God,
YOU are more than my everything. I love your
voice. I love your holy Word. I love your presence. I
love EVERYTHING about you. I'm forever, and
ever more, irrevocably yours.

To Heaven's angels, Daddy and Momma,
The ABSOLUTE, most beautiful, loving, and kindest
parents. I'm grateful for every millisecond we
shared. My heart misses you immensely, but I
know eternity awaits...

To Cynthia and Angela,
The BEST sisters in the whole wide world. I'm
grateful for a bond that outlasts time.

To Arielle and Julianna,
The word 'impossible' loses its meaning when you
BELIEVE in God.

ACKNOWLEDGMENTS

I never imagined sharing one of the most personal and precious things about me – my worship. I kept it private for so long, just between God and me. But I've learned, with the help of others, that my worship unto God is for man, too. Worship is radiant and uplifting. It's infectious and, when ignited, spreads like wildfire. So, for everyone who's ever given me a word of encouragement, just like the Apostle Paul said, *"I thank my God every time I remember you"* (Philippians 1:3).

Thank you, Rev. Cynthia Wilson, for helping me understand and experience true worship and seeing and pulling out something beautiful in me.

Pastors Oshmond Johnson (O.J.), Ken Turner, and James Trivette, thank you for helping me understand the gifts of God and awakening my eyes to all the possibilities.

Jim Anderson, thank you for your readiness and willingness to assist me with my dance moves!

Lisa Landers, my 'angelic' cousin, in every sense of the word. Thank you for your listening ears, encouraging heart, and editing eyes. Your "Go, Jeanette" voice keeps me going.

Audrienne 'Yonnie' Stevens, my worship partner in praise, thank you for understanding me and believing in the God in me.

Christina Davis, thank you for pushing me out of my comfort zone, even when I don't want to move!

Simone Richards, thank you for consistently reminding me it's more than okay to be different and that it's beautifully rewarding to be who God created me to be.

Thank you, Rita Thomas-Golden, for strengthening me, even when you have no clue.

Thanks to Tina Eubanks, one of my biggest writing 'cheerleaders' for cheering me on.

Rhonda Clayton, Semita Wilson, and Arleasa Upshaw, my childhood friends, turned into family. Thank you for your encouragement and our forever friendship — Faces always!

I am grateful for my Sister Circle, a bond forged through pain and loss... strengthened by the unyielding love of God. May we always love well!

Thank you, Word Made Flesh Ministry, for embracing the guidance of the Holy Spirit as we dance through the scriptures together, allowing worship to flow freely. My Disciple Bible class, thank you for stretching me on this walk.

The Kingdom Builders Academy, Tamara Lowe, Zach Lowe, and all the incredible coaches show how to do the right things, the right way, in the right order; thank you. I'm so glad I stumbled across you guys!

And to my family, friends, and all the worshipers... keep worshiping! *I appeal to you therefore, brothers, by the mercies of God, to present your bodies as a living sacrifice, holy and acceptable to God, which is your spiritual worship* (Romans 12:1 ESV).

CONTENTS

Yet a time is coming and has now come when the true worshipers will worship the Father in the Spirit and in truth, for they are the kind of worshipers the Father seeks. God is spirit, and his worshipers must worship in the Spirit and in truth (John 4:23-24).

AUTHOR NOTE

If drawing closer to God has ever stirred your heart, and you are unsure where or how to begin, your search ends here. Even if you've been afraid to go deeper with God, fear not - you are not alone. And for the ones taking their first steps with God, we've been waiting for you... this moment is yours.

Through Jesus Christ, we have access to God... *"I am the way, and the truth, and the life. No one comes to the Father except through me"* (John 14:6 ESV).

One avenue to God is through worship... and it's there that one can experience the peace and solace of God. This book walks you through that lane of worship.

Rediscover the ABCs and let each word, meaning, scripture verse, Bible-related story, and prayer guide you to enter God's presence. Dive deeper into each word as you incorporate it into your daily worship life through each exercise. Write anything that is revealed or anything that you notice, sense, feel, or hear. Get ready to be challenged and inspired as you cultivate a personal relationship with God and pour your adoration for Him through worship.

Come, Holy Spirit, come! Ignite a passion in your people that will never burn out.

Worship is not a chore. It is not a duty or an obligation. But worship is our response to a God who deserves it! Imagine this — you go to the doctor, and they use an instrument to tap your knee. The doctor is trying to see your response or reflex.

What will your knee do? What will happen next? If your knee automatically jerks, then your reflex is good.

When we think of God's grace and mercy, our soul automatically jerks and reacts — it has no choice. It's a natural response. Our body can't contain how great our God is. And that leads us to automatic worship. Some may sing, some may dance, some may shout, some may cry, some may raise their hands, some may fall to their knees, or some may say "Jesus," but all will respond and worship!

Welcome to the ABCs to Intimacy with God, where you and your body will feel things... do things... and say things when you worship. And that's okay. Worship takes us to a different place, where we become different, and that's just the beginning! This might seem like a lot. Exhale. You were born for this. After all, God created you to WORSHIP! Get ready to experience and encounter God like never before.

I'm rooting for you, and countless saints are cheering you on.

EVIDENCE

It was the day that changed my life.

At first, I was in denial of what was happening within me. But now, with the evidence, it was hard to deny. It was even harder to resist.

Every Sunday before I went to church, I would pray and ask God to help me with one thing. Please stop me from crying! During some point in the service, I would always tear up and cry. Sometimes, the tears welled up from the melodic sounds from the choir or the sweet tunes that piped from the organ. Sometimes, they came from the pastor's message of hope and heartfelt prayers.

I had had enough! No more tears streaming down my face. Farewell to the runny and congested nose. I wanted that awkward feeling that I didn't understand to disappear. And then there were these strange movements coming from my body. But yet, what I dreaded most was people looking at me. I wanted no part of it. The only thing I wanted was to be regular. I wanted to go to church and go home. Desperate for a change, I went to the one who could help.

Sunday after Sunday, I prayed. Sunday after Sunday, everything remained the same. But I persisted! As soon as I got home, I would say, "Okay, God, next time." And I was convinced each time that the *next* time would be the *next* Sunday. But it just wasn't working.

I even listened to music while getting ready for service, hoping that everything that needed to come out would come before I left home. But somehow, there was always room for more! Can you say *overflow*?

Nevertheless, I had faith that God would honor my request in my pursuit to stop crying. I did what I only knew to do... I kept praying.

Weeks turned into months, and months turned into over a year. Then came the moment that I had been waiting for. The church service was going great as there were no tears. We were just minutes away from the end of service. The benediction was the only thing standing in the way.

I could hear my heart pounding with excitement. Thump after thump! Yes! Finally, a service without tears. Life was looking good. God had answered my prayer! Thank you, God! Everyone in the sanctuary was standing and holding hands. The preacher slowly began the benediction. I can still hear his words permeating. *"Now unto him that is able to keep you from falling, and to present you faultless before the presence of his glory with exceeding joy, to the only wise God our Saviour, be glory and majesty, dominion and power, both now and ever. Amen"* (Jude 1:24-25 KJV).

And just like that, I felt the tears muster up. Then, the first one fell. They kept falling. I tried to stop them, but it was useless. They were relentless and on a mission. They just kept coming and coming until they all had fallen. At the sound of Amen, I grabbed my purse. I was inconsolable and desperate to escape from the sanctuary. I turned with my head down. I wiped my tears and quickly exited the church.

When I got home, my thoughts were going back and forth on all that had transpired. I tried to comprehend what went wrong, down to the smallest detail. I hoped, no, I expected a different outcome! Unfortunately, I didn't have a clue what happened. All I knew was that this was the same benediction said Sunday after Sunday after Sunday.

Hmmm. Then it hit me! I remembered feeling a soft breeze. There was excitement in the sanctuary. I remember my heart had been pounding with the expectation of not crying. I could smell the aroma of anticipation. But now, it felt like the pounding was coming directly from each word. Somehow, the benediction had wrapped around my heart. Here is the blessing that my ears and heart heard and the response that followed.

Now unto him (Holy are you) that is able to keep you from falling (Thank you, Jesus!), and to present you faultless (Hallelujah!) before the presence of His glory (show me your glory, Lord) with exceeding joy (immeasurable joy), to the only wise God (my God) our Saviour (my Jesus), be glory (YES!) and majesty, dominion, and power, (yes) both now and ever (and ever, and ever, and forever more). Amen.

And on that day, I learned a couple of things. First, never sleep on the benediction. It's at the end of the service for a reason and not just for you to go home. It carries and releases a strong power with enough hope for you to hold onto until the next time.

Next, I realized it was no longer about me. It was no longer what I wanted or didn't want to do. If I cry, guess what? I cry! I cannot hide nor contain my feelings anymore... and I don't want to! What I feel on the inside bursts to come out. I'm so in love with God, and what's even more incredibly heart-stopping is that I feel His love for me. And that, beloved, leaves me breathless! Now I am free. Free from myself. Free to experience God. Free to be a WORSHIPER!

But what is worship? And how do you worship?

The very beginning of true worship is knowing whom you are worshiping. Think back on Jesus' conversation with the Samaritan woman at the well when they were discussing worship. He told her, *"You Samaritans worship what you do not know, we worship what we know, for salvation is from the Jews"* (John 4:22).

Worship centers on God... It's all about Him. Through worship, we respond to, "I AM THAT I AM." Everything *is* because of God... right down to breath and air. However, it's not a one-sided endeavor. We reap the benefits and rewards from communing with Him. In the presence of God, we become enriched as worship releases what He has given us.

Worship comes from the heart. It is the most intimate and personal experience you can have. And by far, the most beautiful. It's an expression of your adoration for God. It manifests a genuine outpouring of our love for ABBA and our steadfast commitment and obedience to Him.

It's from your profound connection with God, where He is present in your life every day... every moment. It comes from spending time – reading, hearing, studying, and obeying God's holy Word, listening intently, hanging on, and *believing every word that proceeds from the mouth of God* (Matthew 4:4 NKJV). It's reaching the place when knowing *about* God is insufficient, but we want to *know* Him unquestionably. To know God is to love God. And to love Him is to obey Him.

4

Worship takes you into the most glorious place. A place of splendor like you've never seen, one that you don't want to leave. It's phenomenal! Worship is our sanctuary. A place we go to be with God – our get-a-way! Our retreat. It's our escape from the chaos of the world to focus on the one who created the world, the one who truly matters. And we bask in His mighty presence, with our hearts beating for more and every second transforming our lives.

We lose "I can't" and "I don't know." And we receive *I can do all things through Christ* (Philippians 4:13 NKJV). We get *with God all things are possible* (Matthew 19:26). And *all things are possible to him who believes* (Mark 9:23 NKJV).

You throw out "I'm not worthy" and you find that you are so loved because *God so loved the world* (John 3:16). And now *you are more than enough... more than conquerors* (Romans 8:37).

It's a place where everything we need is there. It's a place of bliss, and it strengthens us in faith, trust... hope, and joy. Being there refreshes and renews us for the better.

Our love language to God is through worship; we each have our own. Beautiful sounds echo from our hearts to God's. And it doesn't have to be sound. But, through our body movements, our tears, and even in our silence, God hears our hearts. And He responds! Then worship accomplishes its purpose giving all glory, honor, and praise to Him, who is forever more!

Worship happens when you acknowledge God. It can happen at any moment. Sometimes, it just happens. You wake up one morning and start your typical day. You thank God for keeping you through the night. But this 'thank you' keeps going and going. Pure gratitude pours out, and you spend the next fifteen minutes worshiping the Giver and Sustainer of Life. And now you're left wondering where did the time go?

Or, for instance, you are in line at the grocery store, and the old lady in front of you doesn't have enough money for all the food in her shopping cart. She is trying to decide what to put back, but you whisper, "I got it." She smiles, thank you, and heads out of the store with all her items. You immediately feel something that you can't explain. Once you exit the store, you thank God you could help. Your act of kindness was worship. But there's more. You pause, considering that you would've checked out minutes earlier but had to return for *one more thing,* arranging the precise timing for God's glory. And now, it's all about God... Jehovah Jireh, our provider. It's all about our on-time God... *who will make a way.*

Now, suppose one sunny day, you take a walk outside. You notice the beauty in the trees, the flowers in full bloom, the sun that glows, and the warm breeze on your face. Your attention shifts from the beautiful creation, and you acknowledge the Creator for His good work. That's worship.

We were created to worship God. There is no part of life without Him. And when we make Him a part of our lives, it's easy to honor Him. I know, I know, these are subtle examples. But that's where worship starts. At every corner of our lives, we have an opportunity to worship. Every time you exalt God for who He is and magnify Him, you give Him glory and honor. That's worship. When you are obedient to His Word and voice, that's worship. When you give from your heart to someone in need, that's worship.

In 26 lessons, this book will guide you through a deeper relationship with God. You will review and reinforce your understanding of God and faith, love, and commitment to Him. Beloved, if you devote time to Him, He will transform you. You will witness your worship lifestyle explode!

ACKNOWLEDGE

*A*cknowledge is to know or recognize someone or something. Who desires to remain unnoticed or disregarded? Everybody wants to be acknowledged - seen for who you indeed are. And God is no different. Perhaps Jesus said it best. *"Whoever acknowledges me before others, I will also acknowledge before my Father in heaven"* (Matthew 10:32).

God wants us to acknowledge who He is and who He is to us. He's God, and He is my Lord! When we recognize Him, He becomes real. We believe in His existence. We admit He is all that He claims to be.

- He's God – Alpha and Omega, the beginning and the end, the Creator of the Heavens and the Earth.

- He's the Giver and Sustainer of Life - life and breath are in His hands. In essence, He's the One and Only. The Sacred One. The Magnificent One.

- He's El Shaddai, Elohim, El Elyon, and El Roi. He's Adonai.

- He's Jehovah - Rapha, Nissi, Jireh, Shalom.

- Abba is His name. He is Lord. He's Ruler over our lives.

How can I acknowledge God?

We acknowledge what we know. The beginning of any relationship is getting to see that person. By spending time with God, by reading His Word, and with prayer and worship, we learn all about Him. We get to see and feel His heart. We get to have a meaningful two-way relationship.

When we accept God, we receive His authority. We pray to Him, knowing He has the power to do whatever it is we ask. We read His Word to unravel the depths of His existence. With each moment spent reading the Bible and praying, our connection with Him deepens, making Him an integral part of our lives. Our eyes are open, enabling us to behold not only His deeds, but also the very essence of God. We witness His handiwork, and we appreciate it. We share who He is with others.

We get God's attention by acknowledging Him. When we recognize and honor God for who He truly is, glorifying His divine nature... when we utter His sacred name, YHWY, breathing it in and out with every fiber of our being, when we invoke His Word and allow it to flow from us, we start the act of worship. And worship becomes an undeniable connection with God. It becomes our lifeline.

"Because he loves me," says the LORD,
"I will rescue him; I will protect him, for he
acknowledges my name" (Psalm 91:14).

In the Bible...

In the book of Exodus, we find Moses, born a Hebrew Israelite and raised as Egyptian royalty. That is until his conscience collided with the mistreatment and enslavement of the Israelites. The Israelites suffered greatly under the hands of the Egyptians. They cried out to God to deliver them from bondage. God heard their cries and chose Moses as their deliverer. Moses wanted to know God's name. He knew God was the Father of Abraham, Isaac, and Jacob. But he wanted to know the name to tell the Israelites who sent him. And God said to Moses, "I AM THAT I AM. This is what you are to say to the Israelites: I AM has sent me to you" (Exodus 3:14). And because He is, we acknowledge Him. So today, recognize who God is and walk into worship. *Acknowledge.*

God of all Creation, I pray you show me who you are. I want to know the God of Abraham, Isaac, and Jacob. God, I cannot worship who I do not know. I want to know you more, day by day. Please take me back to Genesis, back to the beginning, when you called creation into being. Refresh my mind and heart, God, so I may see you for everything you are. Give me the understanding to answer the question, "Who is the God I know?" And let me hold on to what you show me and acknowledge who you are through every step of my life. You alone are God, and I thank you for all your hands have made. In Jesus' name, Amen.

ACKNOWLEDGE

Revelations

Who is God to you? How can you acknowledge Him in your life?

_____

_____

_____

_____

_____

_____

_____

_____

_____

_____

Take the time to reflect on your writing, then focus on acknowledging God's nature.

This week, record your efforts to acknowledge God throughout your day.

BOLDNESS

*B*oldness is the fearlessness to act - to take a risk. Make no mistake; boldness is not a trait of our own. But it is a power breathed upon us by the Holy Spirit. That fire under courage allows us to do and say the right things at just the right time. We don't have time to think; we do whatever is required. As the Apostle Paul said, *"If God is for us, who can be against us?"* (Romans 8:31)

How can I have boldness?

Boldness is the confidence you have in who God is. That confidence comes when you equip yourself with His Word - reading and studying it. God's Word is our weapon; we arm ourselves with it when we meditate. It's that grit you receive by being in His presence, praying, and worshiping Him.

God wants us to be bold and to come to Him boldly. And so, we pray to Him in boldness, knowing He hears our petition and will respond according to His will. We worship boldly, not just wanting but expecting His presence.

Boldness enables you to testify and declare the wondrous works and the majesty of His name without uncertainty, without fear, without hesitation, and without shame. But with assurance, knowing unequivocally... that He is I AM THAT I AM, the Great I AM. The one who, from dust, formed man. He is the only living God! No one is like Him or superior to Him, and our existence is only because of Him. What a Mighty God He is!

Boldness is the audacity to look wrong directly in the eye and speak to it for what it is – to tell Satan to get behind you. To stand when everyone else stays seated. You don't think about your actions. You respond, knowing and trusting that God is for you, and He is with you.

The Holy Spirit encourages us, and we become brave. Brave enough to step out of our comfort zone and volunteer to pray for someone we see hurting. We become brave to share what God is doing in our lives, making our relationship with Him an open book for all to see.

Boldness is living and speaking God's truth, even if it means persecution or alienation. It is not for people to look at you but to see God, who has given you strength and grace through your words and actions. When we come to God boldly declaring, "Thus said the Lord," a shift happens. God meets us at that intersection of faith and courage, and we experience a spiritual awakening through worship.

Let us therefore approach the throne of grace with boldness, so that we may receive mercy and find grace to help in time of need (Hebrews 4:16 NRSV).

In the Bible...

In the book of First Samuel, we find Goliath, a giant Philistine who terrorized the Israelites. The two armies were fighting against each other. Goliath, however, was looking for a one-on-one fight. And for 40 days and nights, he stood ready, shouting for an Israelite to step forward and accept his challenge - winner takes all. Goliath was defying God's armies. He paralyzed the Israelites with fear, which kept them from responding. Until a young shepherd boy named David came forth. Armed with a sling, five pebbles, and the confidence that God would rescue him, David's boldness defied the odds. With the help of God, all David needed was one shot, and the big, bad giant fell dead. Today, bring your boldness before the Lord and worship. *Boldness*.

Almighty God, I'm so thankful that I serve neither a timid nor shy God. But with all power and might, you, God, are bold. The Earth trembles at the sound of your voice, and hearts crush. When you speak, things happen, and what you declare is done. Everything in Heaven, on Earth, and under the Earth answers to you. Everything is under your feet. Strengthen me in your Word so my foundation is strong, and I can stand on it in faith. Help me believe I can do all things with you. Give me Holy Ghost power so boldness and courage may spring forth. Thank you, God. In Jesus' name, Amen.

BOLDNESS

Revelations

Do you want to be bold for God? Have you ever wanted to speak up but held back?

_____

_____

_____

_____

_____

_____

_____

_____

_____

_____

_____

Reflect on your writing. Ask for divine guidance to be braver in speech and deeds.

This week, keep an eye out for chances to take bold action.

C

---◆---

COMMUNE

*C*ommune is to come together and be with God. It's to share our faith, edifying one another as we focus on the Most High God, who is all things. It's our fellowship with ABBA, our essential time together. David also tells us to, *"Commune with your own heart upon your bed and be still"* (Psalm 4:4 KJV).

Why commune?

We worship God for one reason: to be with Him, to commune with Him because He is God. To be in His presence is everything we need. Being with Him gives us access to His peace, His joy, and His grace. We can sit with Him. We can talk to Him and learn from Him. With more exposure to Him, we gain a better understanding of how and when He speaks to us on a personal level, allowing us to recognize when we are in His presence.

When we are with God, we feel safe in His arms, with a license to be ourselves and share our deepest thoughts. Things we are afraid to speak and utter with our lips are now said from our hearts. There is no judgment, just love. We have the space to be still, to be quiet, and the freedom to get lost in Him. Our imaginations and dreams can officially run wild... blowing into the winds of hope and the endless seas of possibilities!

And God becomes our 'haven,' and we saturate our hearts with His Word, devoting time to study and read. We delve deeper into understanding the meaning of His Word and how to apply it to our lives. Our prayer life becomes enriched the more we are with Him. Stronger. Firmer. Better. What's put in boils over to come out. And now, what is done and said in private becomes a reflection of our lives – it's who we are.

We run into worship when we grasp God wants to commune with us even more than we want to connect with Him. He's been waiting for each opportunity to be with us. Knowing this sends chills throughout our bodies. At that moment, you realize it's just the two of you–God and you. And all He wants is you and your worship. All He wants is us.

When we come to be with God because of our sheer love for God, we get all of God. We have His undivided attention. He's not rushing us off. No way! The Author of Time takes His time with us, giving us everything we need for that moment of WORSHIP. And it's at that intersection of love - ours and God that worship ignites into flames and blazes with intensity.

Behold, I stand at the door and knock; if anyone hears My voice and opens the door, I will come in to him and dine with him, and he with Me (Revelation 3:20 NKJV).

In the Bible...

King David lived in a beautiful cedar house, while God's Ark of the Covenant dwelled in a tent. David wanted to build a house for God worthy of His presence. But God had other plans. In the Book of Chronicles, David gathers all of Israel and shares that God has chosen his son, Solomon, to do the honors. David gave Solomon all the instructions for constructing the temple he had received from God. When the temple was complete, they brought in the Ark. Solomon stood before the altar, prayed, and dedicated the temple to God. Fire from Heaven fell and consumed the burnt offerings, and God's glory filled the temple. And God was delighted with Solomon, telling him his throne would be secure if he communed with Him as his father David did and obeyed His commands. *Commune.*

All loving God, thank you for your unconditional love, for tearing the veil and giving me access to you through your Son, Jesus. Thank you for a space where I can come and pray to you - an open invitation to come to you, just as I am... a safe place to be myself. The more I learn about you and spend time with you, the more my love for you grows and transforms my life. Knowing you, I can understand who I am and what you require of me. I get to experience you and feel your love! It's in that place that I never want to leave. Meet me at that place, God. In Jesus' name, Amen.

COMMUNE

Revelations

In what ways can you connect with God? Meet with Him?

_____

_____

_____

_____

_____

_____

_____

_____

_____

_____

_____

Find a quiet spot and invite God to join you. Be still and bask in His presence.

Take some time this week to be alone with God and reflect on what it feels like to be in His presence.

DESIRE

*D*esire is a strong feeling or want. It's a longing for that which you are after. And that longing, craving, leads you to extreme measures to attain it. *One thing I have desired of the LORD, That will I seek: That I may dwell in the house of the LORD All the days of my life, To behold the beauty of the LORD, And to inquire in His temple* (Psalm 27:4).

How can I receive my desires?

Your heart and God's heart intertwined create a pathway for His desires to manifest. There's absolutely nothing that God doesn't already know. He knows our thoughts before we perceive them... every little thing. Adonai El Roi, the God who sees us. He listens to the beat of our hearts and hears our desires.

God wants us to delight in Him and know Him... intimately. He wants us to desire Him because we sincerely wish to be with Him. It's not rocket science. Nor is it meant to be a one-way relationship. But this desire for God helps us find Him. We put God first. We discover ourselves reading His

Word, grounding ourselves in it and applying it to our lives. The Bible becomes nourishment to our souls. And we read it and feast on His holy Word.

We pray to God from a thirst that only He can quench. And He refills our faith, hope, and trust in Him. By communing with Him, we listen to the sound of His voice for guidance and understanding. We worship God, pouring our affinity and adoration to Him from the songs in our hearts. We long to be in His presence, for our hearts to feel the heartbeat of God. And with each encounter with God, our souls need more and more.

God is the only one that can fill us, the only one who can satisfy us. Now, God's desires for us become our desires – we desire to be in the will of God. Our goal is to lead a life that is holy and righteous. We want to walk in the ways of our Lord through obedience. We long to show love. Experiencing God's presence and savoring His goodness is necessary for us to survive.

When we choose God over all that life offers, when our desire for Him surpasses our wants... and He's no longer what we *want* but what we *need* to exist, then we realize that we do not *want* to be without Him, but we *cannot* be without Him. We discover we need Him every hour. And we choose Him over and over and over again. Worship does not wait – it explodes! It has no choice but to 'be.' And in that place, our desire for Him leads us into worship and keeps us there... not wanting ever to leave.

Whom have I in heaven but you?
And earth has nothing I desire besides you
(Psalm 73:25).

In the Bible...

There were times when Israel was disobedient to God. Times when they showed no love or did not acknowledge Him. They were unfaithful and unrepentant. And God was not pleased. During one of those times, as seen in the book of Hosea, God sent his Prophet Hosea to pronounce His judgment against them. Guilty! Guilty of being corrupt, arrogant, worshiping idols, and ignoring the laws of God. Guilty of lying, murder, stealing, and adultery. And God was ready, all set to unleash His wrath against them. But because He is merciful, loving, and compassionate, He did not carry out His anger against them. God desired love, repentance, and obedience from the Israelites. He wanted them to know Him more than He wished for their burnt offerings and sacrifices. He wanted an authentic relationship with the ones He had chosen. *Desire.*

Most loving Father, your Word says you will give me the desires of my heart. I'm counting on you to do just that. I desire you. I want you, God. You're the one that I am after. I want more of you and all of your love. I love you, God, and I need you every second of my life. I cannot go through life without you, and I don't want to. Fill me with your Word and feed me until I want no more. Remove anything that's preventing our relationship from growing. God, let your desire for me become my desire. Help me run after you, seeking you with my whole heart. Thank you, God. In Jesus' name, Amen.

DESIRE

Revelations

Do you want God in your life? How much?

_____

_____

_____

_____

_____

_____

_____

_____

_____

_____

_____

Close your eyes and talk to God from your heart. Ask Him to ignite your desire for Him.

This week, read Luke 24:13-35. Record what you feel.

EXALT

*E*xalt is to lift up, to praise. *Be exalted O God, above the heavens; let your glory be over all the earth* (Psalm 57:5). The creator of the Heavens and Earth is to be exalted. He is the Lord of Lords and the King of Kings. His name is above every name, and His reign will never end. He's the forever-ever God. He is forever more and forever after. Always. Period. Exclamation Mark!

How do I exalt God?

We exist to exalt God because, simply put, He's everything. We praise God when we come to Him in prayer. That gesture reminds us of who is in control and who we depend on. We pray, attesting He is all-knowing, and we believe He has all the answers we seek. We place all our faith in Him. Our faith says we trust Him with our lives, with every bit of detail. It shows we need Him for guidance. It confirms we can't go through life without Him.

Reading His Word, believing every Word is true, and declaring it back to Him is how we exalt God. We lift God up when we open our mouths and proclaim and profess who the scriptures say He is. When we share what He has done in our lives with others, we bear witness to His power and authority. We acknowledge His divine nature – greatness, perfectness, faithfulness, and holiness.

By obeying God, we exalt Him. Our lifestyle is in line with His expectations – it's in harmony. Being in His perfect will is what we seek. We confess our sins and ask for His forgiveness, which comes only from God. We exalt God when we use our gifts and talents for Him. When we encourage one another in the love of Christ, we honor God. And we lift God higher, and higher, and higher!

Through worship, we show our reverence and adoration for God. With uplifted hands we express our devotion and exaltation to God. As a gesture of deep respect, we bow our heads in honor of Him. Our hearts and all creation sing His praises. He is holy, and we exalt God when we live a godly life. When we are reflections of Him, we mirror His divine attributes. Our light shines and points people back to Him.

When we lift God up, we're thrust into worship. We feel His presence drawing us closer and closer to Him. There's no point in looking for worship. Worship is already there, brimming in the atmosphere, saturating us with His Presence. And we fall right into it, glorifying the Lord of Hosts.

I will exalt you, my God the King; I will praise your name for ever and ever (Psalm 145:1).

In the Bible...

In Psalm 46, we witness God's might and His power. The all-powerful and ever-present God was right there when Jerusalem was in trouble with its enemies. The Israelites had faith in God. They knew they would be alright as long as God was with them. It didn't matter what came their way. God helped them by being everything they needed Him to be — their refuge and their strength. All they had to do was to be still and listen. They rested in His power and received His protection and His blessing. They believed and saw His glory in Israel and among all the Earth. And they exalted Him! *Exalt.*

Lord of Hosts, Heaven and Earth, declare your name. I give you praise, O God. You, O Lord, are Sovereign God, the only Wise God, and your reign is forever from generation to generation. No one can compare to you. No one is greater, and no one is higher. Saturate me, God, in your Word that I may exalt you forever. Teach me your ways so I can tell of your faithfulness all the days of my life. Show me your goodness and mercies that I may declare your glorious works. Keep your Word forever on my lips and in my heart, so I will never stop giving you all the glory and honor you deserve. You deserve it all! You, O Lord, are holy. Holy is your name. Help me, God, to be holy like you. I love you, God, with all my heart. In Jesus' name, Amen.

EXALT

Revelations

Do you worship God? How do you typically engage in worship?

_____

_____

_____

_____

_____

_____

_____

_____

_____

_____

_____

_____

Close your eyes and contemplate God's holiness. Express your thoughts to Him and feel His presence.

This week, ask God to broaden your approach to worship.

FAITH

*F*aith is believing and trusting in God. It's believing in His supernatural power and that He is the Sovereign God. The Apostle Paul defines faith this way: *"Now faith is the substance of things hoped for, the evidence of things not seen"* (Hebrews 11:1 KJV).

Faith is the beginning of our relationship with God. Believing in the accuracy of God's every Word and who He is. It's trusting that He will do just what He says and what He promises. It's knowing He is the same God since the beginning of time. The same today as the days of Abraham, the same tomorrow just like Isaac, and the same forever more as Jacob.

How do I find faith?

"So faith comes by hearing, that is, hearing the Good News about Christ" (Romans 10:17 NLT). It's acknowledging that Jesus is the Son of God. Believing they crucified Him for our sins - that He died and was buried. It's knowing the grave couldn't hold Him and, after three days, He arose with all power.

Every time we read the Bible and hear the good news, it strengthens our faith. The Word gets ingrained in our hearts. And we see God as the God of ALL possibilities. We take His Word literally. *"Truly I tell you, if anyone says to this mountain, 'Go, throw yourself into the sea' and does not doubt in their heart but believes that what they say will happen, it will be done for them"* (Mark 11:23). And we see a wet mountain!

When we genuinely believe that our life looks and becomes different. Knowing that nothing is too hard for our God, we walk with confidence in Him. We live not in fear of the unknown but in the assurance of who our God is. We don't get rattled about things that we can't control. Instead, we pray to the one who controls all things. We live expecting God to show up.

We put all we have in God's hands – our faith, trust, and belief. When we put our faith in God, that faith becomes unshakeable, immovable, and undeniable. That faith doesn't rest on the natural eyes or the present situation. But it takes us into the supernatural, where God is, where the 'impossible' loses its meaning... where the impossible doesn't exist.

It's that faith and belief that there is nothing we cannot do with God, but everything with Him. There, worship becomes our place of rest, where all our hope lies. And *we rest in the shadow of the Almighty* and His presence soothes our souls.

"Jesus said to him, "If you can believe,
all things are possible to him who believes
(Mark 9:23 NKJV).

In the Bible...

Imagine you have suffered from a disease for over twelve years. Your family and community ostracize you because you are unclean. You've used all your money on doctors, yet you still need to be cured. You hear about a man named Jesus who has healed people. And in your mind, you believe He can heal you, too. Jesus is passing through town. You try to get to Him, but there's a large crowd. Determined to get to Him, you press your way through the crowd. You reach for Him, and your fingers barely touch the hem of His garment. But that touch is enough! And just like that, you feel a change in your body, and you realize that touch has healed you. But your body isn't the only one that feels... different. Jesus feels His power flowing and wants to know who touched Him. You confess it was you, and instead of a rebuke, He calls you daughter and tells you your faith has healed you. It...is...*Faith.*

Everlasting God, your Word says without faith, it is impossible to please you. So, God, I ask you to increase my faith in you right now. Help me believe in you and your every Word. Help me put all my trust in you and rely on your Word for my life. Grant me understanding when I read your Word and insight into who you are. Give me hope so I can rise from the low places and count on you and your Word to see me through every situation that life brings. Give me faith, God, the size of a mustard seed, that I will hold on to what you declare and what your Word says, no matter what it looks or feels like. I bless you for faith. In Jesus' name, Amen.

FAITH

Revelations

Who do you believe God is? Who do you say Jesus is?

_____

_____

_____

_____

_____

_____

_____

_____

_____

_____

_____

Close your eyes. Focus on God and follow Him on a faith walk – recalling your beliefs.

This week, ask God to remove anything that challenges your faith, belief, and trust in Him. Then, ask for an increase.

G

---✦◆✦---

GRATITUDE

*G*ratitude is to give thanks and show appreciation - it's all about God and for God. King David reminds us to *"Give thanks unto the Lord, for he is good, his love endures forever"* (1 Chronicles 16:34).

Why gratitude?

There is so much for us to be thankful for in this world. Every second in life offers us a chance to show gratitude to God. Even the thought of the afterlife warrants a Hallelujah praise! But if we start with the basics, life, and breath, there are still not enough words to thank Him for all He has done. When we fail to give God proper due, we miss a chance to see God... and God is everywhere! We miss an opportunity to commune and worship, and that's the best part of God!

God is the reason we exist. He didn't want this world without us–He included us! And not just that, but He made us in His image. And it gets better! He made us a little lower than angels, giving us dominion over everything in the sea, all the birds in the sky, and everything that creeps on Earth. It is a blessing to be known as children of the Most High God.

Thank you, God, for *your* breath! Thank you, God, for entrusting your spectacular creation with us.

King David was right. God is good! He's absolutely amazing. It's just who He is. It's His nature. He embodies strength, generosity, kindness, and love. How great is our God! When we think of His pure majesty, that acknowledgment of His excellence stops us in our tracks to give Him praise and honor. Hallelujah, God!

Our gratitude is for God and to God because of His grace, His mercy, His faithfulness, and His forgiveness. He is an all-in-one God. Everything we could ever need and want is in Him. There is no need to look any further. Our lives are a continuous cycle of expressing gratitude to God through our words and actions. We show Him appreciation for the countless blessings He continuously bestows upon us.

When we come into worship with gratitude in our hearts and upon our lips, we enter a place where it doesn't matter what God has or hasn't done. Our bucket list of wants goes out the window, and even 10,000 tongues are not nearly enough to express our thanks. We enter a posture of gratitude simply because – He. Is. Our. God. And we worship out of our belly as gratefulness gushes out. We give God thanks over and over again.

Give thanks in all circumstances; for this is God's will for you in Christ Jesus (1 Thessalonians 5:18).

In the Bible...

We see that when someone had leprosy, they were unclean, contagious, and couldn't be around people not afflicted with the disease. To be accepted back into the community, they had to show themselves to the priest with a sacrificial offering. In the book of Luke, on one of Jesus' trips to Jerusalem, he encountered ten lepers. They kept their distance and cried out to him for help. And Jesus, compassionate Jesus, told them to show themselves to the priest. They headed off and, on their way, became clean. They had faith in Jesus, as demonstrated by their actions. One, a Samaritan noticed his healing and couldn't contain himself. He started praising God at the top of his lungs. He ran back to Jesus and threw himself at His feet with gratitude running out of him. There were ten cleansed. One came back. *Gratitude.*

Gracious God, I thank you that you are God. I thank you for being all-powerful, all-wise and ever-present. I thank you for your grace and your mercy. I thank you that you are Jehovah Jireh, my provider. Everything I need, you have in abundance! In you, there is no lack. Thank you for your Word, which uplifts my soul when I am down. Your Word encourages me to go on. Thank you for your love that has captured my heart and set it ablaze. I thank you for life, for your breath in my body... for everything you do for me. God, let gratitude never leave my heart or lips. In all I do, help me always give thanks. In Jesus' name, Amen.

GRATITUDE
Revelations

Have you taken the time to think about what you are grateful for? Have you expressed your gratitude to God?

_____

_____

_____

_____

_____

_____

_____

_____

_____

_____

Focus your attention on God and express your appreciation and gratitude.

Remember to thank God throughout your day and specify what you're grateful for.

H

HUMILITY

*H*umility is being modest. God wants us to live our lives humbly and to revere Him. As Solomon states, *"Humility is the fear of the Lord; its wages are riches and honor and life"* (Proverbs 22:4).

Everything is not always about us. We shouldn't need to be at the center of attention. There is no room for people to do things from their selfish ambitions, making it all about them. There is no need to prop ourselves up to make us appear better than our brothers and sisters – making them feel inadequate. No tooting our horns. Nor should we chase after the riches of the world and its power. The motive of what we do comes from our hearts, and God sees both. Pride leads us directly to the fall.

How can one be humble?

Let go of pride.

Acknowledging that we don't possess all knowledge opens the door to learning from others. When we stop listening to the sound of our voice, we can hear what others have to say. When we value opinions other than our own, we become receptive and considerate of others. We can't make people feel less than because of things they don't have or haven't accomplished. But we can treat everyone with respect. As Jesus said, "...*do to others what you would have them do to you* (Matthew 7:12).

When we recognize our flaws, we can grow. When we rely on the confidence of God instead of our own or man's confidence, we realize we are nothing without Him, but we are everything we need to be with Him. Then, it becomes less about us and our abilities and more about God. And the spotlight points to God who rightfully deserves it.

Living in humility is being grateful for what you have. It's putting others' needs before your own. It's being generous with what you have–sharing with those in need. Depending on God and searching for guidance from Him in our lives. God's Word tells us He gives grace to the humble, with promises to bless them... *for they will inherit the earth* (Matthew 5:5).

When we come to worship in humility, not caught up in our abilities or thinking more highly of ourselves than we ought, that's when God can use us and receive our worship. We understand our gifts and talents are not because of us and for us but because of a gracious God, and they are to be used for His glory. Then we can worship God — genuinely humbled that the God of Host made us a little lower than angels.

Humble yourselves before the Lord, and
he will lift you up (James 4:10).

In the Bible...

John the Baptist was different, and the Jewish leaders didn't know what to make of him. They asked if he was the Messiah, Elijah, or a prophet - all to which he said no. But John was clear of his purpose — to prepare the way for the Messiah. And at every chance, he let people know he wasn't even on the same level as the Messiah. And according to John, he wasn't even worthy to untie the straps on Jesus' sandals. After he baptized Jesus, Jesus went with some of His disciples and began baptizing people. A debate occurred with John's disciples and some Jews over ceremonial washing. They noticed everyone was now going to Jesus to get baptized. But that didn't matter to John. John was humbled to be used by God and understood that he must become less so Jesus could become more. *Humility.*

Most gracious and loving God, I pray for humility. Keep me humble at all times in life, no matter the situation. Keep me grounded in your Word so I don't get caught up in myself and live without thinking about others. Help me to do what you require, and that is to love one another. Help me to treat everyone with respect and dignity no matter what. Let nothing impede me from treating people how I want to be treated. I want to be fair. Please help me be more like you. Humble me, God. Humble my heart. Show me the way to humility, that I may walk in it. In Jesus' name, Amen.

HUMILITY

Revelations

Are you humble? How can you show more humility in your life?

_____

_____

_____

_____

_____

_____

_____

_____

_____

_____

Take a moment to review your writing, then have a sincere conversation with God in the areas you need help with.

This week, focus on the areas that were brought to your attention and record the changes you see.

INTENTIONAL

*I*ntentional is to do something deliberately. *Teach us to number our days, that we may gain a heart of wisdom* (Psalm 90:12). I'm sure everyone, at some point, has looked at a clock and wondered where the time has gone. Every day is a gift from God, and we should live every second to the fullest, making it the best we can, unto the glory of God.

What does intentional look like?

We can learn from the best. God is a deliberate God, intentional in all He does. Just look at how He created the world. For six days, He created, was pleased, and rested on the seventh day. Everything He made was purposeful.

Remember when King David wanted to build God's temple? Although God chose David's son Solomon to build His temple, He poured His vision into David. God left nothing to chance. From every measurement to the type of materials and colors used, right down to the weight of gold for each fork, God planned it all.

God wants us to be just as intentional about our relationship with Him. He wants us to prioritize Him above all else in our lives - not just treat Him as an added feature or an afterthought. It's not enough to pencil God in; He desires to be etched in our hearts. Permanently. God wants us to plan to spend time with Him on purpose. Because when we do, it just looks different. It feels different and we do things differently.

We rearrange our schedules, cutting out non-essential things and placing God at the head of our lives. Opening our Bibles, we make time to read and absorb His Word. Meditating on His Word becomes a frequent practice for us. We make it a point to pray without ceasing. We give God thanks continuously. And yes, do we worship!

We include God in our lives throughout our day. So now, He's not just the wake-up to God. But He's the noonday, the evening, and the late-night God. He's every moment and every second in between God. He's constant, ever-present.

Our lives revolve around The Way and doing what Jesus would do. We deliberately treat people with love and kindness. We help those we come in contact with. *Love, joy, peace, patience, kindness, goodness, faithfulness, gentleness, and self-control* become our new DNA.

When we are intentional about coming to God, He deliberately invites us in. And it is there where He meets us. We always have a standing appointment with God where He sees us and takes us deeper and deeper. From the depths of our souls, worship springs forth, glorifying *He who was and is to come.*

So whether you eat or drink or whatever you do, do it all for the glory of God (1 Corinthians 10:31).

In the Bible...

Daniel, a young captive from Jerusalem to Babylon, clung to God's teachings, displaying great integrity and wisdom. He could interpret dreams and visions, and he excelled among supervisors, catching the eye of King Darius, who intended to make him ruler of his entire kingdom. Jealous officials spied on Daniel, seeking accusations, but Daniel was too good. Through the open windows facing Jerusalem three times a day, one could find Daniel on his knees, praying to his God. Officials proposed a law against praying to any but the King for 30 days. They would throw violators of this law into the lion's den. The King signed it. Daniel continued to pray openly, just as he had always done. Despite King Darius' regret, he couldn't reverse the law. And into the lion's den, Daniel went. An anxious King awaited dawn, then ran to the lion's den, calling for Daniel. Daniel answered, emerging without a mark. *Intentional.*

Our Father, who art in Heaven, help me God be more mindful, direct, and intentional about you and my relationship with you. I don't want to be routine or to do things because it's expected or required. But I want to be intentional about you because of my love for you. Help me, God, as I go through life to keep my eyes and focus on you. Help me put you first, above all others — to set aside time to be with you, pray, worship, read your Word, study, and learn more about you. Give me a hunger and thirst for you that only you can satisfy. This is my petition, God. In Jesus' name, Amen.

INTENTIONAL

Revelations

Are you willing to dedicate quality time to God? How can you make that time special?

_____

_____

_____

_____

_____

_____

_____

_____

_____

_____

Close your eyes and focus on God. Let Him know you want to spend more time with Him.

Set aside a time for just you and God. He's expecting you. Record the differences you notice in your life.

JOY

*J*oy is a feeling of contentment. It's a divine state of being. Scripture tells us to be joyful at all times. Nehemiah reminds us, "... *the joy of the LORD is your strength*" (8:10). Joyfulness is not a condition of the heart that depends on how happy we feel. No, this joy is deeper than that. This joy is being content that whatever the situation we are going through, we will get through it.

Where is this joy?

Better yet, how can I attain it?

God is the ultimate source of our joy. We find our joy in God and in no one else. It's that morning joy we wake up with after a dark, restless night... ready to begin our day. It's that loving joy inside our heartbreak when a relationship ends. Tears may fall, but they will also stop. It's that believing joy after losing the job we dedicated our life to. God is our provider who will open another door. It's that trusting joy when the doctor delivers terrible news because we know *the Doctor* who specializes in healing. It's that everlasting joy when our loved ones pass through this Earth to their heavenly home because we will see them again.

Fear, discouragement, pain, loss, and trauma don't have a hold on us. Through it all, the good and the bad, we give thanks to God. Jesus didn't promise we wouldn't have trials in this world. However, He mentioned He has already conquered the world. So, we walk not in defeat, but we continue along in victory. We rejoice at all times.

Oh, Joy! God's gift to us! It comes from our relationship with the Father and our assurance and confidence in Him. It's the place that we rest in, knowing He is our strength.

We receive it by digesting His Word. Faith leads to joy. Prayer brings joy. Trust gives rise to joy. Worship ignites joy. In hope lies joy. Being grateful leads to joy. Joy comes from spending time with God. Loving one another generates joy. Joy is in living a righteous and holy life. Joy is the place where we reside 24/7. We are not part-time or seasonal occupants. No one can steal or take it away. Every day is a good day with the Lord.

When we receive God's gift and live in the fullness of that joy, we enter a place of peace with thanksgiving and security. We understand that we already have everything we need if God is all we have. That empty spot in our lives is now complete and running over, ready to pour out. We embrace joy, and it surrounds us. And joy helps us live out our purpose in life. Then worship takes its rightful place. It manifests!

I have told you this so that my joy may be in you and that your joy may be complete (John 15:11).

In the Bible...

The story of Ruth and Naomi is as beautiful as it is inspiring. In the middle of death, loneliness, and uncertainty, joy comes forth. Naomi's world turned upside down when her husband and two sons died. She found herself alone with two daughters- in-law. Naomi decides to return to Bethlehem and tells the women to return to their mothers. She prays for God to show them kindness and grant them husbands again. After tears and some encouragement, Orpah returns to her mother. But the other, Ruth, was determined to follow Naomi. She left her home country, Moab, to live with her mother-in-law in a foreign country. Ruth was willing to make Naomi's home her home and Naomi's God, her God. Ruth trusted God through the bad and the good and rested in His joy. *Joy.*

God of my exceeding joy, help me not to look to the world for joy. But allow me to understand that joy comes from only you. And it's unto you I look. Nowhere else, God, only you, for you are my source. Fill me up, God, with your joy. Surround me with it, drown me in it, God, so that your joy may be in me, and I may be complete. Let your radiance reign over me right now. Thank you, God, for lifting a heaviness from me and removing any negative emotions that are trying to consume my mind and body and steal my joy. Things that are opposite to your Word and promises you have for me. I declare your joy and peace over my life. In Jesus' name, Amen.

JOY

Revelations

Do you have joy? Who do you look to for joy?

_____

_____

_____

_____

_____

_____

_____

_____

_____

_____

Give your disappointments, past hurts, and failures to God. Focus on Him and ask to experience His joy.

This week, start your mornings by asking God to guide you toward joy and keep a record of the changes you see.

KNEEL

*K*neel is when you rest on your knees. It's a sign of respect, a form of humility. God is Holy, and we kneel in honor of who He is. And as the Apostle Paul said, *"For this reason, I bow my knees before the Father, from whom every family in heaven and on earth is named"* (Ephesians 3:14-15).

Should I kneel?

The spotlight is on the act of being on one's knees. But there are many ways we can show honor to God. Standing tall, we lift our arms high, reaching toward the heavens. Our bodies lie flat on the ground, prostrated, as we submit ourselves completely before God. We can sit with our heads bowed in reverence. We can take our cue from the angels. *All the angels stood around the throne and the elders and the four living creatures, and fell on their faces before the throne and worshiped God* (Revelation 7:11 NKJV). We can plant our faces on the ground or bury our faces in between our knees. Bowing down is another option. The most important thing to remember is that worship starts in the heart, and the verbal and physical become an expression of our profound devotion.

But I believe there's something special that happens when we kneel before our Maker. It can start before we even get on our knees. When we come to God with the mindset, "I'm about to pray," or "I'm about to worship," we have just jump-started our praise. We are coming with a purpose. Our heart races, knowing what's about to take place. Our body knows, too! And it helps us out. Our legs shake as they fall to the floor. Our shoulders lean over, and our heads bow to assume their rightful positions.

We are ready for our prayers to reach God and our worship to extend into the Heavens. We acknowledge there is no one greater than our God. He's it! We bow down to the only Sovereign God, the King of Kings and Lord of Lords. We kneel from a place of surrender – this is unto my God! Our kneeling before the Most High God attests to His reign over our existence. In complete submission, we kneel and give the honor and glory that the One True King deserves.

And we place all our cares and concerns of the world before Him, knowing *It Is Done*. It's in that place where the heart-to-heart conversations take place, where healing comes, where we gain strength, and where we remind God just how great He is.

When we lay all that we are and all we have at His feet, worship rises. That delightful fragrance of our incense reaches into the Heavens and is pleasing before God. The sweetness of worship is beyond words, and it only gets sweeter!

Come, let us bow down in worship, let us kneel
before the Lord our Maker (Psalm 95:6).

In the Bible...

We see kneeling as a symbol of unwavering faith in God. Witness these examples. When the ark of the Lord's covenant was brought into the temple, King Solomon dedicated it to the Lord. Kneeling before the altar of God, with open hands, he prayed to God. Even in exile, Daniel's unyielding faith endured. Three times a day, Daniel's knees kissed the ground as he prayed to God. Stephen performed grand signs and wonders. After they stoned him, his final breath bore a plea from bent knees, asking forgiveness for his enemies. Right after Tabitha, a faithful servant of Jesus, died, they summoned Peter to her house. Peter went into her room, with knees pressed to the floor, and prayed to God. During Paul's farewell to the Ephesian leaders, he knelt and prayed with them. And when Elijah sought rain, he climbed to the top of Mount Carmel. With his face between his knees, Elijah prayed to God. All are reminding us of the power of kneeling before our Maker. *Kneel.*

Merciful God, your Word says every knee will bow before you and every tongue will confess that you are Lord. Here I am, God, with my head bowed. I come before you on bended knees, humbling myself, acknowledging that you, O God, are Lord. I'm not trying to get in a comfortable position, but I bow and kneel out of respect for you. I bow down in the presence of the Almighty, to Him who sits on the throne... to the one who controls the world in His hand. I bow to the only living God. I kneel because I expect an encounter with you when I come to you. And who can stand in your presence? No one. There is none like you on all the Earth, and I honor you. In Jesus' name, Amen.

KNEEL

Revelations

When you pray and worship, do you kneel or bow your head?

_____

_____

_____

_____

_____

_____

_____

_____

_____

_____

_____

Close your eyes. Kneel or bow your head, focus on God's holiness, and feel His presence.

This week, try kneeling and bowing your head and record how it makes you feel.

LOVE

*L*ove is a strong feeling or deep attachment to someone or something. *"Dear friends, let us love one another, for love comes from God. Everyone who loves has been born of God and knows God. Whoever does not love does not know God because God is love"* (1 John 4:7-8).

Is God love?

Yes, God is love. His command of all commands is for us to love Him with every fiber of our being and to love others. And how could we not love Him? Everything about God screams how much He loves us. He sacrificed His only Son to grant us eternal life. Despite our sins, He still loves us and repeatedly forgives us over and over for our faults. He gives us countless chances to get things right and another chance at having another chance.

If that is not enough for you to love God, try spending time with Him. You will not just love Him, but you will fall in love with Him. As you read the *red letters*, they will sink into your soul and melt your heart. His beauty shines through every page, and you will be eager to read more and more and more.

They say you always remember your first love.

Let's pause for a second.

I say you've never known love until you know the Father's love. God's love is beautifully mind-blowing. It doesn't just knock you off your feet but lays you out – it slays! It's so intense it burns through our hearts like a sea of flames. God loves us so much... even thinking about it is just *supercalifragilisticexpialidocious.* (Yeah, that word!)

His love transcends time. It silences and explodes a room at the same time. God has that good, good love. The perfect love. And when we feel His love, our hearts burst to return His love. And love moves between us, through us, and all around us. It's a love so strong that you feel it with every heartbeat. It's so deep that it takes your breath away, leaving you gasping for air.

Just when we think we can't possibly love God more than we already do, He reveals Himself. He comes to us, and we feel His presence. His love floods into us as we pray. We worship, engulfed by His Spirit. We extend and receive love, which brings us back to His love - unconditional, unfailing, forever, and overflowing with mercy and grace. It's so captivating that we embrace love and follow it. We enter worship not just to be *near* Him but to be *with* Him. And we become soaked in the extravagance of His love.

You shall love the Lord your God with all your heart, and with all your soul, and with all your might (Deuteronomy 6:5 NRSV).

In the Bible...

We don't have to look any further than Jesus when we look for love. Created out of love and born to die for love, Jesus is love-incarnated. His mission was not His own, but He completed it out of love. Jesus understood His purpose — to direct people's hearts to His Father and be a sacrificial lamb for man's sins. By doing and saying only the things of God, Jesus showed us the Father's love when He followed God's Word and deeds. He showed us hope and a new life. In His teachings, healings, and resurrections of the dead, we saw compassion and experienced love. And when Jesus' friend Lazarus died, we felt Jesus' love for His friend through His tears. Jesus' crucifixion showed us true love – the kind of love you will lay your life down for a friend. No greater love than this. *Love.*

Precious Father, I thank you for your love that is true... your great love. I thank you for your breath in my body that fills me and reminds me of your love. I thank you that your love will never die, and it will never leave me. Nothing, God, according to your Word, will separate me from your love. Hallelujah! Thank you, Jesus! Thank you for being an example of love and teaching me how to love. Help me follow your lead and to love everyone as you love me. When it might appear challenging to love, let me remember your love for me. Help me, God, to be more like you. Help me live with love front and center in all I do. I love you with everything that is within me. In Jesus' name, Amen.

LOVE

Revelations

How can you experience more of God's love? How can you share that love with others?

_____

_____

_____

_____

_____

_____

_____

_____

_____

_____

Close your eyes and focus on God. Invite God in and tell Him what His love means to you. Stay in that moment. When you are done, record what it felt like.

Tell God daily how much you love Him.

M

MAGNIFY

*M*agnify is to praise God, to extol Him. *Declare his glory among the nations, his marvelous deeds among all peoples. For great is the LORD and most worthy of praise;* (Psalm 96:3-4).

How do I magnify God?

God is superior to everything. He's larger than life – He's God Almighty! To know that we have to know God. So, we read His Word and let it soak into our hearts and minds. And we study His Word and believe. Our eyes are open to His goodness in each scripture, and we can't keep who He is to ourselves. We have to share just how remarkable God is.

We devote quality time to God. The intention behind our praying is to converse with God because we want to fellowship with Him. Our prayer life evolves and progresses before our eyes. Worshiping God is not limited to Sunday mornings – we do it at home too. We experience deep intimate moments with God that are captivating and entrancing in His presence. Our gratitude to Him is constant. We know nothing is too small to thank God for. The slightest thing or remembrance of Him can send us an overwhelming outpouring of gratitude.

The closer we get to God, the more we align with His will. We choose to be obedient because doing anything other than that cheats and taints our relationship with our Heavenly Father. No, we are not perfect, but we strive to be. Will we fall short? Of course, but thankfully, God knows our hearts, and He is a most forgiving God.

Each time we testify about God's awesomeness, He becomes more meaningful. He becomes a part of our lives. We can't get enough of singing His praises. It's almost like when a parent takes their phone and shows you a hundred pictures of little Johnny. Each image has a story that goes along with it... a story of how great little Johnny is. Well, we are a walking picture, complete with our own stories. Stories of how great God is, how He saved us and made a way out of what we thought was no way! Our mind can't comprehend *all* of His greatness. But our mind *knows* that God is great!

When our lives and actions please God, we give Him glory, and we magnify Him. When we come to worship God, magnifying His Holy Name, everything around us is minute. God is the only thing that matters... eclipsing everything else. Then worship becomes both purposeful and gratifying to our soul. It transforms us into His likeness.

O magnify the Lord with me, and let us exalt his name together (Psalm 34:3 NRSV).

In the Bible...

Of all the women on Earth, God chose a young virgin named Mary to be the mother of the world's Savior. Mary and Joseph had already pledged to marry. The angel Gabriel came to her and delivered this miraculous news: she had found favor with God, and He had chosen her to be the mother of His Son. Mary, at first, was afraid and wanted to know how this could be. After all, she was a virgin. Gabriel told her that the Holy Spirit would come upon her, and the power would overshadow her. She would have a son, God's Son. He will be holy and named Jesus. He told her that her cousin Elizabeth, in her old age, was also expecting. Mary was humble and willing, and she believed. Mary went to Elizabeth's house. She greeted Elizabeth, and instantly Elizabeth was filled with the Holy Spirit and started praising God. Mary burst into song, rejoicing and magnifying God. *Magnify.*

O Magnificent God, there is none like you in all the Earth! Heaven and Earth are full of your glory! You are Omnipotent and Omnipresent. Your Word says there is nowhere we can flee from your presence, and I am thankful because I never want to be without you. Not even for one second! God, you are the reason the world exists, the only reason for my existence. You are the Great I Am! I praise you just for being God. You are a good God. You're better than good - you are loving and gracious. Your actions are always righteous, you are a just and merciful God. You are worthy of the praise, worthy of it all. Holy is your name. And I magnify your holy name. In Jesus' name, Amen.

MAGNIFY

Revelations

In what ways can you boast about God? How can your actions magnify God?

_____

_____

_____

_____

_____

_____

_____

_____

_____

_____

For the next few minutes, close your eyes and brag about God.

This week testify to someone about God's goodness.

MEDITATION

We are halfway through our journey to a deeper relationship with God. Breathe. Inhale the love of God.

Meditation and worship pull you into God, bringing you closer to the Creator where you are in oneness with Him. You can hear Him clearer, understand His Word better, and apply it to your life. Meditation brings you into a space of peace.

How do you meditate? Focus is the key. Think about God - His Word, His attributes.

1. Find a quiet place where you will not be disturbed.

2. Invite God in and ask Him to help you understand His Word.

3. Relax your body and mind by breathing in and out several times.

4. From a scripture that you have chosen, read it out loud a few times.

5. Close your eyes and focus on the scripture. (If your mind wanders, refocus by repeating the scripture.)

6. Listen to what God tells you about that scripture.

7. Be open, be still.

8. Before you finish, express gratitude to God.

but his delight is in the law of the Lord, and on his law he meditates day and night (Psalm 1:2 ESV)

NEWNESS

*N*ewness is resurrection. *Therefore, if anyone is in Christ, he is a new creation; old things have passed away; behold, all things have become new* (2 Corinthians 5:17 NKJV).

How can I become new again?

Good news! Christ's death and His resurrection offer us newness in life. Walking in it is possible when we believe, repent, commit our lives to Christ, and change. We are no longer under the power of sin. We are free, dead from sin, and made alive by God. No longer slaves to sin but slaves to righteousness. We have a new Master who forgives our past and gives us a fresh start - a new beginning.

Our outlook on life, things, and events has changed because we now see through the lens of Christ, and we strive to mirror what we see. We've removed the garments that kept us bound in our flesh and wrapped in our sins. No longer are we chasing the things that haunt our past. We bid farewell to our deceptive desires! Corrupt habits are a thing of the past. Judgment and unforgiveness no longer have a home inside us.

The weight of our past actions no longer hangs over us as the old saying, "I remember when," fades away. They are behind us. Things... are... new. Thank you, Jesus!

Our eyes become focused on eternal gain rather than worldly treasures. Patience becomes our rallying cry. Perseverance is our strength. Transformation is our goal. New life, our new beginning. Resurrection power empowers us, and we remain spiritually linked to Jesus Christ forever.

And we gladly clothe ourselves in garments of righteousness, praise, and love. We become changed in our ways, thoughts, values, and lives and are now concerned with the things of God. Things that are pure. Our service to God and others becomes a priority. Love leads us. There is an eagerness and newness in life. That newness leads us to devote time, study, and follow the ways of Jesus. Obey His teachings. We listen and respond to God's will. And we have everlasting victory.

That newness leads us to worship in a new way. We worship from a place of inheritance, knowing we are co-heirs with Christ. Our worship exudes a profound devotion and admiration for our LORD. It leads us to the holiest of holies, a sacred space where we connect with God. We enter extraordinary experiences with our Creator and become enveloped in unconditional love. And worship becomes what we've waited for our entire lives.

Therefore, we have been buried with Him through baptism into death, so that as Christ was raised from the dead through the glory of the Father, so we too might walk in newness of life (Romans 6:4 NRSV).

In the Bible...

Saul of Tarsus was a fierce persecutor of Christians. When they stoned Stephen, a man of great faith who performed signs and wonders, they brought his clothes and placed them at Saul's feet, and he approved. Saul was on a mission to destroy the church. He went inside houses, dragging out men and women and putting them in prison. One day, Saul was on his way to the Damascus synagogues, looking for more people to imprison. A light from heaven flashed around him, and he fell to the ground. Then he heard a voice, and the voice called him by name. Jesus had met Saul on that road, wanting to know why Saul was persecuting Him. Saul's physical eyes were blind, but his encounter with Jesus awakened his spiritual eyes. He followed Jesus' instructions and experienced the vision he saw. Saul received his eyesight, the gift of the Holy Spirit, and newness in life. *Newness.*

Gracious Father, I thank you for being a forgiving God. Your Word says your mercies are new every morning. Thank you for the second, third, and a hundred chances to get things right. I thank you for the ability to change and to become what you have purposed me to be. I thank you for the newness that is coming into my life. As I read your Word, I pray it helps me understand you more and more. The more I know you, the more I will understand myself. Thank you for doing a new thing in my life. I'm ready! I offer my life to you, God; have your way. In Jesus' name, Amen.

NEWNESS

Revelations

Are you ready to experience the newness of God?

_____

_____

_____

_____

_____

_____

_____

_____

_____

_____

Express to God from your heart that you are willing and eager to embrace new experiences with Him.

Write the changes you see.

OBEDIENCE

*O*bedience is doing what you are told. It's obeying God. Jesus said, *"If you love me, follow my commands"* (John 14:15). God wants and expects our complete obedience. After all, He requires it.

What does obedience look like?

The best book ever written is the Bible. It's a roadmap for our lives. The Ten Commandments outline God's laws and requirements for holy living. God doesn't just want us to do what He says because He tells us to. But God wants us to respond to His Word because we love Him.

When we love God, we don't want to do anything but please Him. That love is clear through our obedience, trust, surrender, and reverence. Reading His Word gives us knowledge and understanding, and we consume ourselves with it. Spending time with God helps us develop confidence and deepen our faith in Him. We meditate on His Word, and our ears become attuned to His voice. Intimacy enters as we pray from the secret places of our hearts. We show reverence to God and express our gratitude through worship and praise. We also fulfill our obligation to give back to God by tithing with our gifts and offerings.

Obedience is an act of faith - doing what God tells us to do. To fear God is to do what He requires. When we are obedient to God, it shows in our daily lives. It shows in our relationship with God. We have a firm conviction that motivates us to do what's right. And obedience becomes our cloak and our shield.

Like everything we do, obedience is a heart thing, and God looks at our motives. Are we genuinely sorry for our misdoings? God wants us to obey Him because we love Him. It's not a tradeoff for Him to bless us. But it's to cultivate our relationship with Him. To seal it! Now, we can call Him Lord and Ruler of our lives in our hearts and ways.

We indeed become like children and try to do all in our power not to disappoint God by doing the right things, the right way, for the right reason. Now, there will be times when we fall short, and during those times, we have to rely on God's grace. Lamentations 3:23 reminds us, *"His mercies are new every morning."*

When we come into worship from a heart of obedience, we are no longer just doing an act of worship but *living* worship. What's inside rushes to come out. At this intersection of love and faith, obedience comes. And we worship God in the sanctity of conformity, from purity. Worship flows... effortlessly, and we glorify God.

"What is more pleasing to the LORD: your burnt offerings and sacrifices or your obedience to his voice? Listen! Obedience is better than sacrifice, and submission is better than offering the fat of rams" (1 Samuel 15:22 NLT).

PURSUE

*P*ursue is to go after and chase something. *Flee the evil desires of youth and pursue righteousness, faith, love and peace, along with those who call on the Lord out of a pure heart* (2 Timothy 2:22).

How do I pursue God?

When we want something, we go all in obtaining it. We go after that degree, shutting down the library and studying in the wee hours of the night. We wake up in the nick of time dressed in the same outfit we dozed off in, crust in our eyes, and rush to class. But we get there prepared for that day's assignment.

And that's what God wants from us. He wants us to pursue Him with every breath in our body, mind, and spirit - with all we are. With vigor and determination - go the distance at whatever cost and never give up. Let nothing come between your pursuit — not tiredness and not sickness. Watch out for the roadblocks - distractions conveniently placed in your way. Go around them, through them, or ask God to remove them. Each second, live chasing the only thing that truly matters. God. The pursuit is worth the rewards!

Are you ready? Get set...

Go after God! Study and get to know the God of Abraham. Examine things He did, that He said. Notice His character. Believe Jesus died for our sins. Seek forgiveness. Fast. Pray for wisdom and guidance. Meditate on His promises. Cling to the God who created the heavens and the seas. In the morning, search for Him through His Word. In the evening, listen for His voice. Look for Him throughout the day at every corner of your life.

Pursue righteousness, to be obedient to God. Run into faith to live pleasing before our Maker. Follow love to guide your every step. Search for peace to carry you. Chase after goodness and let kindness spread. Shadow patience and build your endurance. Grab a hold of joy, being ever thankful to the One True God. When we go all in and go after God, seeking Him with our whole hearts, we will find Him.

As we pursue God, that quest leads us to the heart of worship. At that place, our hearts meet the heart of God. The roles have reversed, and the pursuer now becomes the one sought. Then worship pours out from our hearts like water from a running faucet. It does not stop until every drop, every breath, expresses our praise.

You will seek me and find me when you seek me with all your heart (Jeremiah 29:13).

In the Bible...

Esau wanted to kill Jacob when he realized Jacob had cunningly deceived their father, Isaac, and received the blessing that rightfully belonged to Esau. Their mother helped Jacob flee to his Uncle Laban's home until Esau's anger subsided. While he was there, God made him successful in all he touched. One night, an angel told Jacob to leave and return to his native land. Jacob departed in the middle of the night with everything he had amassed, including his family, cattle, and servants. Laban pursued him, and because of a dream from God, he made a covenant of peace with Jacob. Jacob still feared his brother Esau. He sent messengers to Esau to seek his favor. But they returned to say Esau was coming with 400 men. Jacob prayed to God and reminded Him of His promises. That night, Jacob wrestled with a man until daybreak. The man couldn't overpower Jacob, so he touched Jacob's hip socket, which twisted. Jacob realized it was an angel and was determined not to let go until the angel blessed him. And the angel blessed him and changed Jacob's name to Israel — because he had wrestled with God. When Israel saw Esau, Esau ran and kissed him, and the two wept. *Pursue.*

Most High God, I pray that I will never stop pursuing you. Whenever I'm awake, I will look for you. As I go throughout the day, I will seek your face. And not just when I am awake! I want to see you in my dreams! I want to hear your voice. As long as there is breath in my body, I will never stop pursuing you. Just like my body needs oxygen, my soul needs you. Sound the alarm! I want you. I need you, and I am coming after you! You are worthy of the pursuit. To spend a moment with you is better than a lifetime without you. Thank you, God, for being everything I could ever hope for or ask for. I love you tremendously. In Jesus' name, Amen.

PURSUE

Revelations

Are you ready to go after God?

_____

_____

_____

_____

_____

_____

_____

_____

_____

_____

_____

Tell God how much you want Him. Show Him by your actions.

This week, look for ways to include God in your life.

QUENCH

*Q*uench is to put an end to something, to dim. Apostle Paul instructs us. *Do not treat prophecies with contempt* (1 Thessalonians 5:20). Do not deny the supernatural power of the Holy Spirit.

Is it possible to quench the Spirit?

Enter free will.

The Holy Spirit is the breath of God. It's the wind of God. *Ruach.* It bears witness in the Earth, bringing action to God's Word. The Holy Spirit lives inside us to comfort and guide us to the truth. We rely on Him as both our helper and friend. He convicts us and leads us towards righteousness, steering us away from sins. The Holy Spirit inspires our faith in God. He gives us knowledge and understanding. And He imparts us with spiritual gifts to encourage one another and build up the body of Christ. He fills us with power. He *is* power.

And yet, with all that He is, we can prevent the Holy Spirit from doing the work He wants to do with us and through us. And that is called free will - given to us by God. We decide if we want to follow the unction of the Spirit. It's up to us if we want to do what He tells us to do. The choice is all ours.

We quench Him when we hold untrue beliefs about Him or attribute our strength to something other than Him. When we refrain from spiritual emotions, we diminish Him. We impede His work when we deliberately disobey Him. When we ignore His power, we suppress Him and restrict what He does through us. When we stifle the Holy Spirit, we grieve Him. We hinder His work when we become embarrassed to follow His lead or afraid to do so because of what people might say or think.

The Holy Spirit is the fire we want to keep burning –to inflame, engulf, and intensify! We never want it to go out. When the Spirit leads us, we may not easily understand or make sense of things. We might even question what we heard. But what truly matters is our willingness to heed His prompting and act obediently. We bow when He instructs us to bow. If He stirs us to run, we take off. If He says to deliver a message, we speak that message. We surrender to the Holy Spirit, allowing Him to use us for His glory.

When we worship, determined to be led by God's Spirit, then we go wherever the Holy Spirit leads us. We worship in faith and not in fear. Surrounded by a million people, all we can see is the beauty of God. We release our worship to *Him who is forevermore* and rivers of living water stream forth. And we become fully engulfed in the mighty presence of God!

Do not quench (subdue, or be unresponsive to the working and guidance of) the (Holy) Spirit (1 Thessalonians 5:19 AMP).

In the Bible...

Before Jesus ascended, he told his apostles not to leave Jerusalem until they received the gift promised from God—the baptism of the Holy Spirit. And on Pentecost, the Holy Spirit came. People started speaking other languages, while others thought they were drunk. Peter boldly explained that this is what Jesus promised and the prophet Joel prophesied. Peter witnessed to the people, and about 3,000 repented and got baptized that day. The apostles performed signs and wonders. And the people believed, prayed, and fellowshipped together. They sold what they had and gave it to those in need. Ananias and his wife Sapphira sold a piece of their property but kept some proceeds. When Ananias gave the apostles the rest, Peter asked why he deceived the Holy Spirit by keeping some of the money. Ananias fell dead. His wife came, and Peter asked her if that was the price they paid for the land, and she said yes. Peter asked how she could plot to test the Holy Spirit. He told her the men who buried her husband would now bury her. And she fell dead. The same men carried her off and buried her next to Ananias. Fear seized all who heard. *Quench.*

O Lord our God, your Word says your sheep know your voice and follow you. God, help me understand when and how you communicate with me. Help me hear you clearly and to learn your voice. As I read your Word, let it come alive in my spirit. Help me, God, so that the deceiver won't succeed in tempting me. Make yourself known to me so that I can discern your presence from others. God, I do not want to quench your precious Holy Spirit. Please forgive me for the times when I did. Help me not to run from your Spirit but to embrace it. I want to follow you and do what you tell me to do. Use me, God, for your glory. Help me respond boldly for your honor. In Jesus' name, Amen.

QUENCH

Revelations

Do you quench the Holy Spirit? Do you grieve Him?

_____

_____

_____

_____

_____

_____

_____

_____

_____

_____

_____

_____

Close your eyes and ask God to help you hear and feel Him.

This week, pay close attention to the Holy Spirit.

REVERENCE

*R*everence is a deep love and respect for someone. *It is the Lord your God you must follow, and him you must revere. Keep his commands and obey him; serve him and hold fast to him* (Deuteronomy 13:4).

How do I show reverence to God?

Throughout the Bible, it declares God is holy. Book after book, scripture after scripture, verse after verse, repeats His divinity. It acknowledges His sovereignty. And I'm a believer.

We revere God because He is holy. His wonders are beyond our understanding and leave us amazed. One look at the world is just astonishing. God is mesmerizingly glorious. He's beautiful! Who can measure up to Him, to His Majesty? No one, that's who! We are in plain awe of God! We revere God because we respect Him for all that He is. And we fear Him with the same breath because we love Him.

Just like the Israelites did, we also learn about God to see what He requires from us. We read and study His Word, looking to understand Him. We observe what He likes and what He doesn't. And we take note of His faithfulness. We obey the commands that He set forth from the beginning of time. By praying, we reinforce our bond with Him. Following His voice, we journey down the path He has set before us. We remember His holiness, and we keep His Sabbath.

True reverence is a lifestyle we live from our hearts, choosing holiness and what's good. We know disappointing God is more than we can bear. So, we walk in faith. And we keep God close. It's more than what we do, but how we do it. We genuinely forgive others when they hurt us and ask for forgiveness from others. We help those in need and serve them with kindness and respect, not just for show.

Authentic reverence inspires our worship. It's personal. YHWY is the God of all the Earth. But He is my God, and He is my Lord. I am forever loved by Him. I am forgiven by Him. He talks with me and sits with me. He holds me close, His arms enveloping me in a sweet embrace. I am His. And my heart adores Him.

We revere God when we call upon His name and give Him thanks and praise. When we come to worship in reverence, honoring He who sits on the throne, our worship bursts from an overflow of our love and awe for Him. Worship is exhilarating! It's a taste of Heaven on Earth.

Therefore, let us be grateful for receiving a kingdom that cannot be shaken, and thus let us offer to God acceptable worship, with reverence and awe (Hebrews 12:28 ESV).

In the story of Job, we see suffering and perseverance. Job was different, blameless, and upright. He feared God and despised evil. With seven sons, three daughters, thousands of cattle, and servants at his service, Job had it all. Now Satan was roaming the Earth, and God asked if he had considered Job. Satan said if Job lost all he had, he would curse God. And God permitted him to test Job, but he couldn't lay a finger on him. One by one, tragedy after another, Job lost everything — his oxen and donkeys, sheep and servants, camel and all ten children. Yet, Job didn't charge God with wrongdoing. Satan told God that if Job's life were on the line, he would surely curse God. God again permitted Satan to test Job, but he couldn't kill him. Satan afflicted Job with sores all over his body. Job's wife told him to curse God and die. But Job didn't sin. With a broken piece of pottery in hand, he sat in the ashes and tended to his wounds. He revered God, and God restored everything that he lost. *Reverence.*

O Majestic and Beautiful God, how Magnificent is your name! God, your Word teaches me to revere you and to fear you. I recognize your holiness and honor you. You are the One True God, and I adore you. You are the Only Wise God, and I respect you. Your Word is sweeter than honey to my lips and pierces my heart and soul. May I live a life that is both holy and pleasing to you. Let my words and my actions honor you. Help me respect your laws and obey them. There is only one God, and YOU are the one. I give you all the glory and praise. I love you forever. In Jesus' name, Amen.

REVERENCE

Revelations

In what ways can you show reverence to God?

_____

_____

_____

_____

_____

_____

_____

_____

_____

_____

_____

Think about God's holiness and worship Him.

Let God know you revere Him. Show Him in your actions.

SURRENDER

*S*urrender is to give up your will and control. Then Jesus said to his disciples, *"Whoever wants to be my disciple must deny themselves and take up their cross and follow me"* (Matthew 16:24).

How do I surrender?

There's no limit to God's love for you. It's infinite. Because of His love, He wants the absolute best for you. It's just one thing. Life is better when we are in the complete will of God.

Have you ever wanted something so bad you tried doing everything you could to have it? But nothing worked. The more you tried, the farther out of reach it became. The stars just weren't aligning in your favor. Our desires are not always God's desires. But when we surrender to God, we align ourselves with Him. His desires become our desires, and it sets us on a different course.

Surrender is an act of obedience and faith. It's trusting God completely. We let go of our control, and we give power to God. We acknowledge God as the source of our life. And we yield to His way, not knowing His plans but believing in Him. *For I know the plans I have for you," declares the LORD, "plans to prosper you and not to harm you, plans to give you hope and a future* (Jeremiah 29:11). We give up what we want. Our 'yes' to God starts our new journey, and our lives take a new direction. Our path is not the same. We stop chasing dead-end desires. We bypass 'my way or the highway.' Plans that lead us away from God are in the rearview.

We say yes to God's will, yes to His way. And that's the place we live in, following the will of our Father. Surrendering unlocks the keys to an obedient life. It may not be easy, but it is worth more than gold. We vow to lead a righteous and holy life. Our minds are no longer tormented by conflicting thoughts and emotions... no longer pulled and tugged. Just like Jesus instructs us to pick up our cross daily, we must surrender daily to God. We wake up and permit God to have His way. We make ourselves available to be used by God for His glory.

When we surrender to God, we say hello to our new life. We follow where He leads, and His purpose becomes our passion and reveals the answers we seek. Worship intensifies when our *yes* meets *His will*. It's at that place where worship becomes purposed driven by not your will but by the will of God. And worship freely exudes.

Do not be conformed to this world, but be transformed by the renewal of your mind, that by testing you may discern what is the will of God, what is good and acceptable and perfect (Romans 12:2 ESV).

In the Bible...

Jonah was a prophet chosen by God to go to Nineveh and preach against their wickedness. Jonah, however, boarded a ship and sailed in the opposite direction. God sent a violent storm upon the sea. To reduce the weight, the sailors threw some of the cargo overboard. The captain went below deck where Jonah was sleeping, telling him to get up and call upon his God to save them. The sailors cast lots to see who was responsible, and of course, the lot fell on Jonah. Jonah told them he was a servant of God and was fleeing Him. He suggested they throw him overboard. They tried rowing back to land but couldn't. They prayed to God and with no other choice, threw Jonah overboard. Immediately, the sea grew calm. God had a giant fish swallow Jonah, who was in the fish's belly for three days and nights. Jonah prayed to God, and the fish spit him out on dry land. And God told him again to go to Nineveh and deliver His message. Jonah went. He surrendered and obeyed God. *Surrender.*

My rock and my fortress, my God, my King. O Lord, you are life. You are my life. Apart from you, I cannot do anything. Help me to surrender not to my wants but to your ways. Give me the strength to trust the plans that you have for my life and the courage to live up to those plans. Help me follow you, Lord, and give my life entirely to you for your glory. I want what you want for me. I want to be what you have purposed me to be. No inhibitions. Your will. My life is yours; have your way, God. Take charge. Take control. I surrender, and I give my life to you. In Jesus' name, Amen.

SURRENDER

Revelations

Have you fully committed yourself to God?

_____

_____

_____

_____

_____

_____

_____

_____

_____

_____

Ask God to search your heart and reveal any obstacles that may be hindering you.

Invite Him into all areas of your life and permit Him to take control.

TRUTH

ruth is the Word of God. Jesus said, *"If you hold to my teaching, you are really my disciples. Then you will know the truth, and the truth will set you free"* (John 8:31-32).

How can I know the truth? How can I live there?

God is the truth. His every Word is pure. From Genesis to the Book of Revelation - the beginning to the end, God unveils who He is, book by book. God cannot lie, and that's the whole truth – the absolute truth. When we read His Word, we find the truth of who God is and who His Son is. His Word leaps off the pages and into our hearts. That truth becomes a seed planted in us. It's a part of us. Every time we study, we water it, and it grows.

We believe!

We pray God's Word back to Him, reinforcing us with truth. We meditate, and the insight becomes more precise and more transparent. The closer we get to God, the more we want to know. There are new questions that arise. New perspectives that we receive. And our Heavenly Father does not disappoint. He reveals Himself in more ways.

God's truth speaks to us. His truth is life in our bones. It's a fire that burns our souls. It pierces our hearts and encapsulates our minds. And every moment in His Word takes us deeper and deeper with God. Our ears are open to hear God's voice. We see God right before our very eyes. And we feel Him. God's truth is our life belt! It's our ticket to eternity. It heals us, frees us, releases us, and restores us. We die to sin. We experience forgiveness. Hope is at our door... and we open it!

When rooted in His Word, we hold on to what was true thousands of years ago. And truth, along with obedience and faith, is our recipe for living. We are not afraid of the truth and we don't fall to lies and deceit. But we stand on the Word of God because we know it will never fail. We abide by God's Word. And we live by the truth according to the teachings of Jesus. It illuminates our path, and we walk in His truth. God is always present. *Never will I leave you; never will I forsake you* (Hebrews 13:5).

When we come to worship in truth, the Spirit of God leads, and it absorbs us in His power. When what we say, our words are what we believe, we worship in truth. ABBA's love radiates through us, lifting us up, and bringing us into His presence. It's beautifully majestic. It's invigorating! And we worship from oneness with God the Father.

Teach me your way, O Lord, that I may walk in your truth; unite my heart to fear your name (Psalm 86:11 KJV).

In the Bible...

Zacchaeus was a chief tax collector. He was very wealthy, no doubt from the very ones he collected money from. Jesus was passing through Jericho, and Zacchaeus wanted to see Him - just one problem. Zacchaeus knew his height wouldn't allow him to see Jesus over the crowd. So, by climbing a fig tree, Zacchaeus got a better view. When Jesus came near him, Jesus looked up and saw him and told him to come down because He had to stay with him. That was music to Zacchaeus' ears as he hurried down the tree. People mumbled Jesus would be a guest at the house of a sinner. Zacchaeus said he already gave half of his possessions to the poor and would give them four times that amount if he had defrauded anyone. The truth set Zacchaeus free, and he received salvation from Jesus. *Truth.*

O Righteous God, I know the way to you is through your holy Word. Your every Word is truth. What you say... becomes and is so. Instill your truth and hide your Word in me, especially in my heart. Help me learn and understand all about you. Keep my mind on you, where I can't get enough of your Word. But I look to your Word to give me life and to sustain me. Your Word is food to my soul. It is the blueprint for my life - my benefits, insurance, and healthcare policy. It's my 'how-to guide' to navigate through life. You are the truth that leads me into all righteousness. Allow your truth to permeate my soul, so I always stand on your Word. This is my request. In Jesus' name, Amen.

TRUTH

Revelations

Does the truth scare you? What does God's truth mean to you?

_____

_____

_____

_____

_____

_____

_____

_____

_____

_____

_____

Close your eyes and focus on God. Ask God for wisdom when reading His word.

Study God's truth and allow it to penetrate your soul.

U

UNINHIBITED

*U*ninhibited is to be free and to express yourself without constraints. God is God, with no restraints. He is completely uninhibited. That's precisely how He wants us to be about praising and worshiping Him - without restrictions. *Praise the LORD, my soul; all my inmost being, praise his holy name* (Psalm 103:1).

What does uninhibited look like?

Uninhibited looks like singing as if no one can hear you or dancing like nobody is watching. The caveat is you don't care if anyone hears you or sees you. We become free when we release that fear of our flesh and our hearts focus on God. We are so caught up in ABBA that responding to Him, to His goodness, becomes second nature. Our praise and worship are for God and to God. It's never to please people. God doesn't want us to be concerned, influenced, or intimidated by what others might say or think.

Praise lifts God up. We praise God with songs, prayers, and testimonies. We praise Him when we obey Him, love and serve others. It's all about acknowledging and giving God thanks for who He is and what He has done for us. Whether corporate or individual, it's about you and God. It's our happy place – full of excitement and rejuvenation. But the moment your mind thinks about God's deity, the atmosphere shifts. You immediately feel the weight of His holiness and cannot stand in His presence.

Worship bows down to God, beginning where praise leaves off. From our hearts, an abundance of love for ABBA rushes through. And now it's *only* about God. He is all that matters. We worship God from the depths of our souls... and time stops. We become entranced with Him. And we surrender to the overwhelming power of the Holy Spirit. Where He goes, we follow.

Spontaneity has a new home, and it goes into the unknown. There is no thinking happening. We just go with the flow of God. Pure, unadulterated praise! Abandoned. Unhindered and boundless worship! We understand King David better. From all our might and everything within us, we give it to ABBA. And we experience the glory of God — outward and inward.

At that intersection of freedom and love, worship erupts! It becomes more profound than we could ever imagine. Unexplainable things happen, things that you never thought possible when you give in to the Spirit. And that feeling... you will never forget, which leaves you running into worship again and again.

Now the Lord is the Spirit, and where the Spirit of the Lord is, there is freedom (2 Corinthians 3:17).

In the Bible...

To the Israelites, the Ark of the Covenant represented God's presence. The Philistines had taken it as a trophy, and then sickness came upon them. After seven months, they returned it. Next, it rested at Abinadab's house for 20 years, and David attempted to return it to the City of David. But Uzzah, Abinadab's son, touched it when the oxen that were pulling the cart stumbled. God's anger flared, and Uzzah died immediately. They took the ark to Obed-Edom's home, which was nearby. It remained there for three months, bestowing blessings on the entire family. David realized he hadn't sought God before he moved the ark the first time. He had the priests, and the Levites consecrate themselves. He gathered all of Israel, and they cheered. At the sight of the ark approaching, David danced from his heart with all his might unto God. But David's wife was furious with how David danced and dressed, saying he was undignified. David declared he would be even more undignified for God. *Uninhibited.*

God of Heaven, your Word says whom the Son sets free is free indeed. May you liberate my heart, God. Free my mind. Free me from the bondage and remove all restraints put on me by man and myself. In Jesus' name, remove all restrictions that keep me from you once and for all. Help me not to be afraid of experiencing you. Free me up, God! So, I may walk in freedom and not fear accomplishing what you have for me. Nothing will hinder me from being who you have called me to be. May my worship, praise, prayer, and study of you be unrestricted and unencumbered. Thank you, God, for setting me free. In Jesus' name, Amen.

UNINHIBITED

Revelations

Is there anything preventing you from being free?

_____

_____

_____

_____

_____

_____

_____

_____

_____

_____

_____

Focus on God and worship Him like no one is watching!

Do it again and again and again.

V

---♦---

VESSEL

*V*essel is a person used by God, a container. *Has the potter no right over the clay, to make out of the same lump one object for special use and another for ordinary use?* (Romans 9:21)

How can I be a vessel?

God created us in His image and formed us to be His vessels in life. When we are open and willing, God fills us with His Holy Spirit to accomplish His work. And when God's agenda becomes our priority, we have the extraordinary task of participating in His work here on Earth.

There is nothing in this life we can do on our own. We can't even breathe without God. His generosity knows no limits, as He supplies us with all that is necessary. He pours into our bodies, our containers - giving us everything we need to do the work He has set for us. The gifts others receive from Him do not bother us. We are grateful to be used in any capacity He so desires.

Our hands, now extensions of His, can accomplish mighty works, all for His glory and honor. We serve others. Selflessly. Our giving extends beyond material things, but we also sacrifice our time for others. And when directed, we lay hands on the sick, and they recover.

Yes, we are God's vessels!

We are His mouth, the mouthpiece of God, speaking and declaring His Word that brings life and salvation. We share the Gospel of Jesus Christ. He shines through us so people may see Him more clearly. Our testimonies are stories upon stories about how great God is, offering hope and a new life. Our plea is for people to repent and get baptized. And we lead people to Christ so they may accept Him as their Savior, as their Lord - trusting and turning their lives over to Him.

We are His feet, ready to go where He sends us – to the prisons, the lost and abandoned, the sick and the poor, the highways and byways, reaching all along the way. *And you will be my witnesses in Jerusalem and in all Judea and Samaria, and to the end of the earth* (Acts 1:9).

When we come to worship, God can use us when we come as open vessels ready to do His work. Out of our devotion and adoration to God, we empty ourselves in the presence of the Almighty. But don't worry. Worship becomes our filling station, a place to refuel to carry out the work of God. And God's Spirit graciously replenishes us.

> *Therefore, if anyone cleanses himself from the latter, he will be a vessel for honor, sanctified and useful for the Master, prepared for every good work (2 Timothy 2:21 NKJV).*

In the Bible...

Saul, a fierce persecutor of Christians, encountered Jesus on the road to Damascus and became physically blind for three days. He didn't eat or drink, and his companions led him around. Jesus appeared to one of His disciples, named Ananias, in a vision. Ananias answered Him. Jesus told him to go to Straight Street to lay hands on Saul from Tarsus. But Ananias had concerns as Saul's reputation preceded him. Ananias tells Jesus that Saul had harmed His holy people and that he was coming to Damascus to do even more harm by arresting believers. Jesus told Ananias to go, and He said Saul was His chosen vessel. Ananias did what Jesus said. He went to the house, laid his hands over Saul's eyes, restored his eyesight, and baptized him with the Holy Spirit. *Vessel.*

Loving God, I want to be used by you and for you. Sanctify me, God. Use me for your glory, God. Let my life make a difference. Use me, God, according to your riches and glory — to accomplish your will here on Earth as it is in Heaven. Teach me, show me God, and fill me with your Holy Spirit. Here are my hands. Take them to do your work. Guide my feet, God, to follow you, to go where you say I should go. Have your way with me, God. Whom shall you send? Here I am, God, ready to be used by you. I am your vessel and your instrument. Send me God! In Jesus' name, Amen.

VESSEL

Revelations

Do you want to be a vessel for God? Do you sense God trying to use you?

_____

_____

_____

_____

_____

_____

_____

_____

_____

_____

Close your eyes and focus on God. Ask God to use you for His glory.

Record your assignments.

$\mathcal{W}$

WILLING

$\mathcal{W}$illing is being open and not forced to do something. *Be shepherds of God's flock that is under your care, watching over them – not because you must, but because you are willing, as God wants you to be; not pursuing dishonest gain, but eager to serve* (1 Peter 5:2).

How can I be willing?

Willing is when your 'want' connects with your 'spirit,' leading you to a desire to do something. It's that 'yes' that comes from your heart and your mind. It's not because of ritual or obligation. But you sincerely desire to do so. God wants us to come to Him willingly. He wants a genuine relationship with us, not forced. He wants us to be willing and not grudging participants.

When God is in our lives, we choose to live a life gratifying to Him - and we can't get enough of Him! We open our Bibles to read and the scriptures fly off the pages and into our hearts. We meditate to uncover divine revelations in the mysteries of God. And each time, God takes us deeper, dazzling our minds. We apply those teachings to our lives daily to honor Him.

We obey His Word because our hearts do not want to disappoint Him. We pray out of necessity, not for show. But because our soul desperately needs Him... to feel alive. We give from our heart, even from our lack. We know our blessings ultimately come from God, and everything we have is already His.

Our *willingness* to God charts our new life. We become available to be used. Our ears are open, eagerly awaiting the whispers of God, guiding us to the opportunities that lie ahead. And we are ready. We go, not knowing the path our feet will tread, but willing to walk into our destiny. We believe in the one who sends us—not knowing where it will lead, but agreeing to go the distance, *come what may.*

Gratitude fills our hearts, and praise is continuously upon our lips. We look forward to voluntarily sitting at the feet of God, relishing the overwhelming feeling of being in His presence. We look forward to listening to His every Word and soaking up His knowledge and profound wisdom.

When we bring that openness to worship, at that intersection of 'willing' and 'yes', our physical eyes connect with our spiritual sight. The Heavens open up, and we *behold* the majesty of God... we *see* God's glory! Worship is not *to die for* but to *live for.*

Restore to me the joy of your salvation, and sustain in me with a willing spirit (Psalm 51:12 NRSV).

In the Bible...

Isaiah was a great prophet. After the death of King Uzziah, Isaiah was in the temple, and he had a vision of Heaven. He saw the Lord in all of His glory sitting on His throne. Seraphim, angelic beings, were flying around and proclaiming God's holiness. The doorposts shook from their angelic voices. Smoke filled the temple. This was no ordinary vision, but Isaiah was in the presence of God, experiencing God Almighty. Isaiah saw his life in ruins because his lips were unclean, and his eyes had seen God. Then, touching his mouth with a live coal, one seraph took his guilt away. Then God spoke to Isaiah, asking whom He should send. Isaiah, willing, responded to God to send him. *Willing.*

My God and my King, let my yes be yes and come from my heart. Let it come because of my love for you. Keep me in your Word so my love for you never leaves. But with every breath, may it grow stronger and stronger and keep me wanting more of you. I believe your every Word and your plans to prosper me and not to harm. I trust your plans for my future. My future is with you. My now is for you, and I will do your will. I want to please you, and my soul wants to please you. And just like Isaiah, my answer is yes. Use me, send me God. I love you. In Jesus' name, Amen.

WILLING

Revelations

Are you willing to follow God? To go where He sends you?

_____

_____

_____

_____

_____

_____

_____

_____

_____

_____

_____

Close your eyes and focus on God. Let Him know you are available and willing.

This week immerse yourself in God's Word.

XTRA

*X*tra is more, in addition to. *Whatever you do, work at it with all your heart, as working for the Lord, not for human masters, since you know that you will receive an inheritance from the Lord as a reward. It is the Lord Christ you are serving* (Colossians 3:23-24).

How can I receive more? Do more?

God is the gift that keeps on giving and giving. His Word is life, and it prepares us for life. When we use His Word as a blueprint for our lives, we have everything we need. We have 'xtra' because God is more than what we need.

The more we read God's Word, the more we receive from it. Reading it regularly will increase our appetite for it, making it pleasing to our souls. We don't read it just out of obligation but because we have an insatiable appetite for it and we can't get enough!

By studying and meditating, you can gain insight into the wonders of God. God reveals even greater things when you give Him your full attention. You ask for wisdom, and He graciously gives it to you, and your understanding sharpens. You apply His Word to your life and live a more abundant and fruitful life.

The more time you spend with God, the more you want Him in your life. Your spiritual senses heighten. You become aware – in tune to listening for the voice of God. Your eyes see things differently. You develop the attributes of God – to be holy because He is holy. You become a neighbor... to all. Your servant's heart goes above and beyond what's required. There is "xtra" that you give, not concerned with earthly treasures but building up spiritual riches.

Your heart receives gratification each time you help someone in need. When you pray and intercede for others, your life is the one that is blessed. Every prayer strengthens your relationship with God. It increases your faith and deepens your intimacy with Him. And God places additional people in your path, presenting you with more opportunities to pray.

When we worship, God doesn't just get a part of us. He gets *all* of us. With every encounter, He replenishes our souls, His very essence lingering in our thoughts, urging us to seek Him further. We get *xtra*! Worship transports us into the throne room of God's grace, where His peace and love flood us. We get the overflow.

If anyone forces you to go one mile, go with them two miles (Matthew 5:41).

In the Bible...

Sometimes in the Bible, we see where God requires more. When someone requests you go one mile, go two miles. If someone takes your tunic, then give your cloak as well. If someone slaps you on one cheek, turn and give them the other cheek. Even when we want to be fishermen, He wants us to be fishers of men. These are all 'xtras' that God wants of us. Ten virgins were preparing to meet the bridegroom. They went off to meet Him and brought with them ten lamps. Now, five of the virgins brought oil along with the lamps. The other five only brought the lamps. It was nightfall before the bridegroom arrived. The virgins who brought xtra oil prepared in advance. But the others who didn't bring oil had to leave to search for more. They missed the bridegroom. *Xtra.*

Glorious God, your Word says whatever I do, I should do it for your glory... doing it with everything within me. Help me always give my best to you - the best of my time, worship, offerings, gifts, and best self. Help me be generous in all I do and for that generosity to come from my heart. Let me rise to do more - the more I read your Word, the more I learn about you, the more I want to do the right thing, the more I pray, the more I worship, and the more I want you. I'm here for more of you, God, and all the xtra! Give me 'the more' God! In Jesus' name, Amen.

XTRA

Revelations

In what ways can you search for more? Do more?

_____

_____

_____

_____

_____

_____

_____

_____

_____

_____

_____

Close your eyes and focus on God. Ask God to show you 'the more' He wants from you.

This week look for opportunities to do more.

𝒴

---❖---

YEARN

𝒴 earn is a deep longing for God. It's an intoxicating desire for God. *My soul yearns, even faints, for the courts of the LORD; my heart and my flesh cry out for the living God* (Psalm 84:2).

How can I yearn for God?

The allure of God is spellbinding. Every time we read the Bible, we become struck by the beauty of His Word. Time and time again, our eyes open and see there is nothing God won't do for those He loves... and our hearts melt. We see the richness of His grace and mercy and undying devotion. And we know not even *eternity is the limit!*

We *believe* He is Lord God Almighty. We read, and we read. God's Word is a hypnotic melody that enchants our senses. We *study*, and we learn. We *meditate* on His Word, and it gets infused in our souls. And there's nothing better! *How sweet are your words to my taste, sweeter than honey to my mouth!* (Psalm 119:103)

We pray to communicate with God and spend time with Him. There is a restless hunger and thirst from deep within that only God can quench. *As the deer pants for streams of water, so my soul longs after You, O God* (Psalm 42:1). His thoughts are essential. To fulfill our purposes, we must have direction and an understanding of them. We devote our lives to live according to the Giver and Sustainer of Life. We live by His Word in faith and devout obedience.

And you are *desperate* for God. It's intense and all-consuming. A mere glimpse of Him is not enough. You desire His entire essence - you need it to breathe. Your entire being craves God... to be in His presence. And your soul and heart aches for Him. His voice becomes a symphony that resonates deep inside. You can't get enough. You want Him more than anything. Where He is - is where you want to be. Nothing else can satisfy this desire within you. Nothing... else... will... do.

Experiencing God's presence in worship is truly electrifying. It's like a magnetic force instantly connects your heart with God's heart, imbuing you with agape love. At that moment, you feel a complete oneness with God. His presence is so powerful that you become frozen in awe... unable to move or speak. Worship feels like stepping into a calming river that effortlessly carries you along. His Spirit gently touches you, and His Presence immerses your soul, leaving you drenched and refreshed. It's truly a mystical experience that goes beyond the limitations of language.

I yearn for the Lord, more than watchmen do for the morning, yes, more than watchmen do for the morning (Psalm 130:6 NET).

In the Bible...

David was a King who loved God. He was a man chasing after God's own heart. David's connection to God was rooted in his deep love for God. He trusted God and centered his life around Him. He publicly displayed his profound love for God and was not ashamed to adore and revere Him. God's Holy Spirit led his worship. David danced. He sang. He played the harp and lyre. David lived in God's presence, and his worship was God-focused. With all that he did, he did unto the glory of God. Beautiful Psalms after Psalms spilled out from his heart. Within them, we see an incredible hunger in David's heart, satisfied only by God. We hear the sounds, the beating of his heart, and panting for his God. And we feel his insatiable desire burning to be near God. *Yearn.*

Most Beautiful God, my soul thirsts, and my entire being craves for you. Where you are, I want to be... in your presence, Lord. Fill me with your Word. Saturate my mind and my heart in your Word. Let your Word pierce my soul as I read it and study it. May it come alive when I pray. May it explode in and through me when I praise your name! I want to see you, God. I want to feel you too. Give me more and more of you - more of your presence. I want you, God; my heart longs for you alone. Hear my prayer, God. Show me your glory; show me your goodness. In Jesus' name, Amen.

YEARN

Revelations

Have you ever felt a burning in your heart for God? For His Word? His presence? Do you want to experience this?

_____

_____

_____

_____

_____

_____

_____

_____

_____

_____

Close your eyes and focus on God. Ask God to feel His presence.

This week let's take another look at Luke 24:13-32.

$\mathcal{Z}$

ZEALOUS

$\mathcal{Z}$ealous is to be eager for God. As the Apostle Paul points out, *"It is fine to be zealous, provided the purpose is good, and to be so always, not just when I am with you"* (Galatians 4:18).

How can I be zealous about God?

Good News! God is looking for people to be zealous for Him. He is looking for people to be relentless in reading and studying His Word. He wants us to be eager to learn His Word and not just skim through the pages. But to take our time – studying for clarity and understanding so we can share the good news with others and make disciples.

God wants a total commitment from us. A commitment to follow Him, to be faithful and obedient, persistently doing things the right way - His way. God wants us to be just as zealous in our giving and serving of others. He wants us to give our all to Him, withholding nothing, but always looking for ways to advance His kingdom. He wants us to be zealous for the Law and to live in righteousness with *the belt of truth around us.*

When your commitment to God meets your passion for God, you enter an ardent state. You are keen to go the distance for God, whatever it takes, no matter the sacrifices. But you will do whatever it takes to serve God wholeheartedly. Your life is not your own. You live for God and God alone! You exemplify loyalty and devotion in all your actions, never faltering in your commitment to ABBA. God's defender!

When you are zealous for God, your worship takes a different stance. Your strategy is a one-two punch. You are both willing and eager - ready to empty yourself before God. You worship from a place of reverence, believing and trusting God's every Word. Not only are you open to meeting with God, but you are eagerly expecting the encounter. And you wait, like a kid in a candy store, for His presence to enter the room and completely saturate you.

You worship fervently, entirely captivated by the grandeur and magnificence of His holiness. The intensity roars throughout your soul like a powerful gust of wind. Turning the ground beneath your feet into hallowed territory. Your worship becomes holy ground because God is there... meeting with you. (Flashes of Moses and a burning bush that doesn't burn come to mind.) Your body responds the only way it can, bowing before the *One True King*, acknowledging He is Lord... the Great I AM!

Never be lacking in zeal, but keep your spiritual fervor, serving the Lord (Romans 12:11).

In the Bible...

When Saul was persecuting Christians, he did it with zeal. He was enthusiastic about wreaking havoc in their lives. Saul pursued them with vigor, going into their homes and dragging them out. He even asked the priests for letters permitting him to arrest them. And the priests gave him the authority. Not only did he persecute Christians, but he also did it legally. Saul changed when he encountered Jesus on Damascus Road, but his zest remained. He received a new name, Paul, and he refocused his zeal. Handpicked by Jesus, he experienced both the grace and mercy of God. Instead of persecuting Christians, he became their teacher, sharing the gospel of Christ with them. Paul dedicated his life as a servant of God, going the distance... even to his death. *Zealous.*

God of wonders, stir up your Holy Spirit and start a fire within me. Set me on fire! Let my heart burn when I read and study your Word. Your Word is power, and your Word is life to all who hear. Open up the scriptures to me so they will be active. Help me to commit myself to you. Help me to be eager to obey your Word, eager to live a life according to your Word. May this fire never die out. Let my bones feel your flames. Consume me, Almighty God! Give me strength as I seek to do your work – whatever the cost. I live for you, God, and I hope I make you proud. In Jesus' name, Amen.

ZEALOUS

Revelations

How can you be eager to learn about God? To do His work?

_____

_____

_____

_____

_____

_____

_____

_____

_____

_____

_____

Ask God to ignite a passion in your soul for Him.

For the rest of your life, spend time with God. Get to know Him through His Word. Direct your attention towards Him and WORSHIP!

ABOUT THE AUTHOR

Jeanette Williams is not your ordinary believer, but a fiery soul ignited by her unwavering devotion to God. With a heart ablaze for worship, she is a force of nature after God's own heart. As a passionate storyteller, she dances through the scriptures, infusing her love and devotion through movement and melody, captivating hearts.

Jeanette's communion with God transcends mere words. In the sacred space of worship, she finds a language that surpasses human comprehension, opening doors to realms of spiritual intimacy that few have dared to venture into. In her presence, you can almost feel the very heartbeat of God resonating within you, enabling you to experience the power of worship in ways you never thought possible.

Whether you're seeking a speaker who can stir your soul, an author who can transport you to new spiritual heights, or a mentor who can help you unlock the fullness of your faith, Jeanette is the transformative force you've been waiting for. She embodies authenticity, vulnerability, and deep empathy. She understands the struggles, fears, and distractions that can hinder our connection with God, and she empowers individuals to break free from them.

Through workshops and retreats, Jeanette's ability to usher you into the presence of God have made her a beacon of light for those seeking a deeper connection with God. Join her on this extraordinary adventure of the spirit, where the ordinary becomes extraordinary, and your relationship with God reaches new depths. Prepare to be moved, inspired, and forever changed.

Jeanette Williams... guiding you into a world of worship, connection, and unbridled spiritual passion.

It is my heartfelt prayer that this book brings you closer to intimacy with God.

I'd love to know which alphabet resonates with you the most. Kindly contact me at jeanettewilliams1231@gmail.com. In return, I'll send you a gift.

If you've enjoyed this book, please leave a review on Amazon.

Also, please visit my YouTube page for meditation videos: @JeanetteWilliams-df5nx.

Godspeed!

www.ingramcontent.com/pod-product-compliance
Lightning Source LLC
Chambersburg PA
CBHW070721130626
46553CB00005B/2097